Philosophy's Cool Place

ALSO BY D. Z. PHILLIPS

The Concept of Prayer

Moral Practices (with H. O. Mounce)

Faith and Philosophical Enquiry

Death and Immortality

Sense and Delusion (with Ilham Dilman)

Athronyddu am Grefydd

Religion without Explanation

Dramâu Gwenlyn Parry

Through a Darkening Glass

Belief, Change, and Forms of Life

R. S. Thomas: Poet of the Hidden God

Faith after Foundationalism

From Fantasy to Faith

Interventions in Ethics

Wittgenstein and Religion

Writers of Wales: J. R. Jones

Introducing Philosophy: The Challenge of Scepticism

Recovering Religious Concepts

Philosophy's Cool Place

D. Z. Phillips

Cornell University Press

Ithaca and London

First published 1999 by Cornell University Press

Cornell University Press strives to use environmentally responsible
suppliers and materials to the fullest extent possible in the publishing
of its books. Such materials include vegetable-based, low-VOC inks
and acid-free papers that are recycled, totally chlorine-free, or partly
composed of nonwood fibers. Books that bear the logo of the FSC
(Forest Stewardship Council) use paper taken from forests that have
been inspected and certified as meeting the highest standards for
environmental and social responsibility. For further information, visit
our website at www.cornellpress.cornell.edu.

Printed in the United States of America

Library of Congress Cataloging-in-Publication Data
Phillips, D. Z. (Dewi Zephaniah)
    Philosophy's cool place / D. Z. Phillips.
       p. cm.
    Includes index.
    ISBN 0-8014-3600-1 (cloth : alk. paper)
    1. Philosophy, Modern.   I. Title.
B791.P43   1999
101—dc21   98-50653

Cloth printing   10 9 8 7 6 5 4 3 2 1

FSC FSC Trademark © 1996 Forest Stewardship Co
SW-COC-098

In Memory of

RUSH RHEES

My ideal is a certain coolness. A temple providing a setting for the passions without meddling with them.

—WITTGENSTEIN

Contents

Preface

The title of this book, *Philosophy's Cool Place,* is not meant as an adjectival acknowledgment of the pleasures of spending every spring in southern California. Rather, it refers to my attempt to elucidate a contemplative conception of philosophy, one indicated in the quotation from Wittgenstein that serves as a motto for this book. A contemplative conception of philosophy raises fundamental questions about the nature of reality and the possibility of discourse. We are asked to give a certain kind of attention to our surroundings without meddling with them. It seems to me that this conception of philosophy is central in Wittgenstein's work and in critical extensions of it by Rush Rhees.

I have dedicated this book to the memory of Rush Rhees, not simply because of my debt to him as my teacher but also for reasons directly related to the present work. I am indebted to discussions with Rhees in my attempts, in the first three chapters, through comparisons of Socrates, Kierkegaard, and Wittgenstein, to elucidate a contemplative conception of philosophy. I have developed the contrast between Kierkegaard and Wittgenstein begun in "Authorship and Authenticity: Kierkegaard and Wittgenstein," published in a special Wittgenstein issue of *Midwest Studies in Philosophy* (1992) and reprinted in my collection *Wittgenstein and Religion,* Macmillan and St. Martin's Press, 1993. These further developments were stimulated by James Conant's response to me, "Putting Two and Two Together: Kierkegaard, Wittgenstein, and the Point of View for Their Work as Authors," in *Philosophy and the Grammar of Religious Belief,* edited by Timothy Tessin and Mario von der Ruhr in the series *Claremont Studies in the Philosophy of Religion,* Macmillan and St. Martin's Press, 1995. My understanding of a contemplative conception of philosophy was formed also through my editing of Rhees's work, in particular his *Wittgenstein and the Possibility of Discourse*, Cambridge University Press, 1998.

In the remainder of the book, with the exception of the autobiographical afterword, I discuss, with reference to the work of Richard Rorty, Stanley Cavell, Annette Baier, and Martha Nussbaum, how extremely difficult it is not to go beyond a contemplative conception of philosophy. The chapter on Rorty consists, more or less, of my "Reclaiming the Conversations of Mankind" published in *Philosophy*, 1994. I am grateful for permission to use the material here. When I looked for a treatment of values with which to contrast that of Rorty, it was to Rhees that I turned. I had discussed Rorty more extensively in *Faith after Foundationalism*, Routledge, 1988, and Westview paperback, 1995.

My interest in Cavell's work is long-standing, but the present work was stimulated further by reviewing Richard Fleming's *The State of Philosophy* and writing a critical notice of Stephen Mulhall's *Stanley Cavell: Philosophy's Recounting of the Ordinary* in *Philosophical Investigations* 17, 2 (1994) and 19, 1 (1996), respectively. The contrasts I drew with Cavell were also informed by editing Rhees's work, not only the work already mentioned but also Rhees's *Wittgenstein's "On Certainty," Philosophy and the Presocratics*, and *Plato and Dialectic*, all hitherto unpublished.

My work on Baier and Nussbaum grew out of two McManis Lectures given at Wheaton College in 1996. The work on Baier appears in a somewhat different form in *Critical Reflections on Medical Ethics*, edited by Martyn Evans, JAI Press, 1998. I am grateful for permission to use the material here. In the contrasts I wanted to draw in relation to Baier's work, I had in mind Rhees's *Moral Questions*, to be published by Macmillan. Rhees's use of literature, along with my discussions and those by Peter Winch, R.W. Beardsmore, and Ilham Dilman, constitutes a Wittgensteinian tradition with which I contrast Nussbaum's appeals to literature.

The autobiographical afterword grew out of an invited address delivered to the Pacific Theological Society at Berkeley in 1997.

I am extremely grateful to Helen Baldwin, secretary to the Department of Philosophy at Swansea, for preparing the typescript for publication and to Timothy Tessin for help with the proofreading; to Roger Haydon for being an encouraging editor at Cornell University Press; to Nancy Raynor for outstanding editing; and to the Press's anonymous reader for helpful suggestions.

D. Z. PHILLIPS

Claremont, California, and Swansea

Philosophy's Cool Place

1 Philosophical Authorship: The Posing of a Problem

The nature of philosophy is itself a philosophical problem, a problem as old as philosophy. It is a problem that can arise from many different directions, and this book explores simply one of them—the problem of philosophical authorship.

What is a philosopher trying to do? What is the subject matter that is characteristically his or hers? These questions cannot be answered by a survey of what philosophers actually do. Whatever one concludes about the nature of philosophy, there will be philosophers who, as a matter of fact, engage in something different. Is one to say that they are not doing philosophy? If one does, one will be accused of operating with an a priori conception of the subject. When one looks at the variety of activities that go on under the name of philosophy, any attempt to reduce these activities to an essence, or a definition, in any descriptive sense, is obviously futile.

On the other hand, philosophy is a critical discipline, and much of its history has been concerned with its own nature. The discussion of that concern will not be content with a purely descriptive answer of the kind we have mentioned, if only because philosophers are critical not simply of the conclusions other philosophers may reach but also of what they take themselves to be doing in philosophizing.

In this book, I discuss what I call a contemplative conception of philosophy, one that is concerned, in a certain way, with giving an account of reality. There is a big difference between philosophers who want to keep this conception of the subject and those who either never possessed it or who, for one reason or another, think it is a conception that must be abandoned. Some abandon it gladly, others with regret.

Where one stands on these issues will affect what one thinks a philosophical author is doing.

Philosophers may have a contemplative conception of the subject and yet arrive at conclusions that others, who share the same conception, disagree with strongly. The contemplative character of their concerns is shown not in the conclusions they reach but in the *kind* of questions they raise, the depth of their treatment. Thus the fact that we disagree with a philosopher's conclusions will not be a sufficient reason to say that that philosopher was not wrestling with central issues in the subject in a contemplative mode. This disagreement does not mean that one is indifferent to the conclusions but rather that one can learn in this context, where one does not when philosophers cease to engage, in this contemplative way, with fundamental questions in the subject. The disengagement may take the form of a too easy skepticism: the denial that there is any reality to contemplate. Or the disengagement may take the form of a denial that philosophy's primary task is one of contemplation and understanding. Philosophy's task, one may say, is not to contemplate reality but to answer substantive questions about it or to bring about changes in it where necessary. This latter conception of philosophy suggests itself easily to a technological culture with its primary interest in arriving at answers and solutions. In this book, I try both to characterize the questions raised by a contemplative conception of philosophy as well as to show why, given that philosophers have pursued such questions in different ways, a certain development of them is to be preferred, philosophically, over the others. This conclusion is not stipulative, for it must be supported by philosophical argument.

I realize that in speaking of the contemplative conception of the subject I run the risk of associating 'contemplation' with contemporary vulgarizations of the concept, where it is thought of as an easy, unearned serenity, to which working through, or struggling with, difficulties would be quite foreign. The philosophical contemplation I want to discuss, by contrast, demands a *kind* of attention to our surroundings that we are reluctant to give them because of the hold which certain ways of thinking have on us. These ways of thinking have us captive, not against our wills, but because of them.

The attention philosophical inquiry asks of us becomes an issue as soon as we say that philosophy is concerned with giving an account of reality. The thought may strike us: aren't the other arts and sciences concerned with the same thing? When science, history, literature, and the social sciences are said to pursue certain tasks, what task remains for philosophy to fulfill? It is tempting to conclude, the most general question of all: "What is reality?" or "What is the reality of all things?" The difference between philosophy and other inquiries, on this view, is a difference in generality. Just as biology is a more general inquiry then botany or zoology, so, we may think, philosophy is the most general discipline of all. Philosophy is not concerned with the reality of this and that but with the nature of reality as a whole. When we look back to the beginnings of philosophy among the pre-Socratics, is that the conception of philosophy we see at work? The fact that they inquired into the nature of 'all things' shows that they were asking a question that cannot be answered by empirical means. There is no empirical inquiry into *that*. Any empirical investigation will be into a specific state of affairs, no matter how general. Any hypothesis put forward in this context, that takes the form 'It is ...' allows the possibility of a counterthesis, an 'It is not ...'. But the 'It is ...' that is supposed to be an account of 'all things' is an account of reality; it does not allow the possibility of 'It is not ...'. An account of the nature of reality is supposed to rule out the question, "And why do you call *that* real?" The philosophical account of reality is not meant to explain the existence of one state of affairs as opposed to another but to show how it is possible for anything to be real. But given this feature of a philosophical account, the answers offered by the pre-Socratics seem problematic.

The pre-Socratics give us various accounts of the nature of 'all things'. Thales says, "All things are water." Pythagoreans say, "All things are number." Democritus says, "All things are atoms." And so on. They all had special reasons for giving the answers they did, but these reasons are not my primary concern. Rather, I want to draw attention to a difficulty that attends all such answers, a difficulty almost as old as the answers themselves: the problem of measuring the measure. An account of reality is supposed to rule out the further question, "And what about the reality of *that*?" Yet this is the question which the pre-Socratic answers seem to invite. If Thales tells us that water is the nature of all things, it is natural to ask what account is to be given of the water. How can one rule out such an account? The difficulty is not confined to Thales' answer but will apply to *any* answer that claims to offer *the* measure of 'all things'. The problem is, what account is to be given of 'the measure'? And one can ask this of *any* measure offered.

Plato appreciated the problem of measuring the measure. He came to see that the account of reality being sought, the account of 'all things', is not one that the natural sciences can provide. The issue is not an experimental one but a logical or conceptual question that can be settled only by *discussion*. Take the question of the reality of physical objects. Observation or experiment may determine whether a *particular* physical object exists, but the reality of physical objects cannot be discussed or determined in the same way. To begin with, in any attempted empirical explanation, we would be presupposing the very reality we are supposed to be investigating. But that is not the kind of account Plato sought. The question is whether anything intelligible can be said about the reality of physical objects, whether a coherent account can be given here. But even if an account can be given, it would be an account of the reality of physical objects. Can a similar account be given of reality as such—an account of 'all things'?

The problem of measuring the measure can easily lead us to abandon the search for an account of 'all things'. We might say, "There are particular measures of this or that, but there is no measure of all things." When this is said, the view is not that there *happens* to be no measure of all things but that it makes *no sense* to seek one. Such a conclusion would have a direct effect on what we take to be the scope, content, and nature of philosophical authorship. If accepted, the conclusion would be that a philosopher *cannot* investigate, in any positive way, the nature of reality.

We can see how this conclusion is reached by linking the problem of measuring the measure to the related difficulty of subliming the measure. If we face a plurality of measures, why should we favor any *one* above others as *the* account of the reality of 'all things'? For example, 'the mathematical' has been said to be the measure of 'the real', not only by the Pythagoreans and by Plato but also, in the twentieth century, by A. J. Ayer, when he said that it was logically inappropriate to speak of 'certainty' in connection with any empirical proposition. Why should 'the mathematical' be so favored? Why should the fact that there are important differences between mathematical certainty and my certainty that I am writing these words in the familiar surroundings of my home lead to the assertion of certainty in the former context and its denial in the latter context? Other philosophers have sublimed, as a measure of certainty, incorrigible sense experiences, which are said to be 'the given' from which each of us, necessarily, has to begin. The problem thus created is how, from such beginnings, we can have any confidence that we share a common world or how there *can* be a common world to share. Again, given important differences between "I am in pain" and "You are in pain"—for example, the first, unlike the second, is not based on observation—why should that fact lead to the conclusion that while I am certain of my own agony, I can never be certain of yours?

If we combine the difficulty we have called "the problem of measuring the measure" with the difficulty we have called "the problem of subliming the measure," why not settle for recognizing that there are many measures of 'the real', that what we *mean* by 'the real' is not one thing but varies with the contexts in which questions about 'the real' may arise? Protagoras would have been happy with that conclusion, as in the twentieth century would J.L. Austin, who insists that when we speak of 'the real', we should always ask, "A real *what?*" It seems that philosophy has been brought down to earth with a vengeance. It can no longer claim to be the unique means by which *the* nature of reality is arrived at.

If we reach this conclusion, what are its implications for philosophical authorship? Philosophy, it seems, is left with a purely *negative* task, as far as metaphysics is concerned. It has the task of exposing its pretensions. Metaphysics loses its subject—there is no reality to discover, inquire into, or give an account of. In some people's eyes, this negative task leads to the demise of philosophy. In other people's eyes, including my own, this consequence is not a necessary one. The negative task may, and has, led to different conceptions of philosophy. But those conceptions would not be what I have called a contemplative conception of philosophy. I want to elaborate on these two consequences.

The Sophists said there was no such thing as 'reality'—nothing to inquire into in the way the pre-Socratics had thought. But the Sophists went further, positing that there is no such thing as 'knowledge' or 'truth', only *opinion*. Opinions may be strong or weak, but not valid or invalid; they may be effective or ineffective, but not true or false. Their strength and efficacy depend on the degree of public backing they receive. Words are weapons, and rhetoric is the means by which weak opinions can be changed into strong ones, and vice versa.

Needless to say, if we accept this view, we accept not simply the demise of a contemplative conception of philosophy but also the demise of philosophy itself. Small wonder that while Callicles acknowledged that philosophical argumentation may sharpen a young person's wits, he argued that those wits, once sharpened, would be better employed in helping one to get on in the city. It would be scandalous to devote one's life to philosophy. Philosophy, at best, should be the handmaid of rhetoric.

Abandoning the pre-Socratics' search for an account of 'all things' need not lead to the demise of philosophy or to the extremity of the Sophists' conclusions. After all, Socrates, who also abandons the pre-Socratic search, nevertheless provides a devastating critique of the Sophists. But I want to ask what conception of philosophy Socrates arrives at. My conclusions, in this respect, are tentative, but even if I am wrong about Socrates, the noncontemplative conception of philosophy I attribute to him is certainly in evidence in the subject.

Socrates asks Gorgias what it is that he teaches. The question seems to be straightforwardly factual but goes to the heart of philosophy. Socrates is really asking whether there is anything to teach, whether there is a *logos* in things to be understood. Gorgias claims that his subject has to do with speech; but, he is asked, "Speech about *what?*" If Gorgias gives a substantive reply, Socrates points out that the subject is that of an already existing art, such as mathematics, music, medicine, shipbuilding, or weaving. If each art has its distinctive subject matter, what distinctive subject remains for the so-called art of rhetoric? Neither is there any refuge for Gorgias when he claims that rhetoric is not concerned simply with speech but also with speaking *well*. Once again, Socrates asks, "Speaking well about *what?*" Whether one is speaking well will be determined by the logos appropriate to the art relevant to the example of speech. The most rhetoric can be, Socrates argues, is an aid to expressing what there is to understand in the various arts—arts that cannot be reduced to rhetoric.

Socrates shows that rhetoric cannot be an art and that it is logically parasitic on the very 'knowledge' and 'truth' whose reality the Sophists denied. Persuasion involves a reference to 'truth', because persuasion, even when deceptive, involves a reference to 'what is the case'. The persuader relies on concepts of 'truth' and 'knowledge' in those he is trying to persuade. In that way, Socrates inverts the claims of the Sophists: the arts and their logoi cannot be reduced to rhetoric; rather, rhetoric is logically parasitic on what it denies.

But, by the same Socratic questions, can we have a contemplative conception of philosophy? What if Gorgias asked Socrates to specify philosophy's subject matter? Socrates might say that he is concerned with discourse. But, then, Gorgias could ask, "Discourse about *what?*" Once again, any substantive answer, on the Socratic view, will be the domain of an already existing art. What if Socrates were to say that he is concerned with knowledge and understanding? Could not Gorgias ask, "Knowledge and understanding of *what?*" Any substantive answer leads back to the arts. Are we thus to conclude, that philosophy, like rhetoric, is not a genuine art, because it has no distinctive subject matter?

We need not embrace this conclusion, for there is an essential difference between Socrates and the Sophists. The latter are not even aware of the problems with which Socrates is wrestling, confident that they have all they need in their persuasive techniques. When asked what kind of discourse he is concerned with, Socrates could have replied, "Discourse about discourse." He is concerned with the *possibility* of discourse, the possibility of 'knowledge' and 'truth'. His question is whether an intelligible account can be given of them, the kind of account that can be arrived at only through a conceptual discussion. The question, however, is whether Socrates' conclusions express a contemplative conception of philosophy. I am inclined to think that they do not, although my reasons for saying this will depend on the degree of irony I ascribe to Socrates.

With respect to the nature of reality, Socrates said that the only difference between himself and others is that he knows that he does not know. If I take this remark as being free of irony, Socrates would be saying that it *should* be possible to give an account of reality as a whole but that he, unlike others, knows that no one has succeeded in providing one. Furthermore, Socrates comes to the same conclusions in more restricted contexts, such as questions about the nature of knowledge or the nature of virtue. When given examples of 'knowledge' and 'virtue', Socrates denies that these can constitute the nature of knowledge and virtue, presenting counterexamples to prove it. This procedure annoyed Wittgenstein. He thought the examples Socrates was offered were perfectly acceptable. They are rejected only because Socrates thinks that all examples of knowledge and virtue should have something in common, that 'knowledge' and 'truth' should have an essence. Thus on the first reading of Socrates, he is skeptical about the possibility of a successful contemplative account of reality.

On the other hand, if I attribute irony to Socrates' remark, he is saying that he knows that he does not know what others take for granted so confidently—that is, he knows that there is nothing to know here. There is no nature or essence of reality to be discovered, hence it cannot be the subject matter of philosophy. One may ask why irony is necessary. If this is what Socrates means, why doesn't he say so? Why doesn't Socrates produce a direct refutation of his opponents? These questions misunderstand Socrates' mode of inquiry. He does not think that a direct refutation of an opponent is possible in philosophy. Such a refutation would suggest that the opponent's thesis was intelligible but false. Yet the trouble with such theses is not their falsity but their unintelligibility. An attempt is made to say something that does not make sense. Socrates can get someone to see this only indirectly, by getting that person to appreciate the route that led to the confusion, so that the person no longer wants to say what he or she did.

On the nonironic reading of Socrates, he is skeptical about whether we can give a successful account of reality as such. If we ascribe irony to Socrates, he is questioning the intelligibility of such an account. Instead of trying to give an account of reality as such, we will be content to clarify the confusions in the attempts to do so and to point out the diverse uses of 'real' to be found in the various arts. It is futile to seek a conception of reality that transcends these contexts.

Having contrasted the reactions of the Sophists and Socrates to the recognition that the *kind* of account of 'all things' offered by the pre-Socratics is not a possible one, what are we to say of Plato? He, too, shared their negative reaction to the pre-Socratics, but he did not think that the attempt to give an account of the nature of reality should be abandoned. For Plato, Socrates' reaction is, in some ways, dangerously close to that of the Sophists. If we do not attribute irony to Socrates, he is skeptical of the possibility of giving an adequate account of the nature of reality, whereas Plato wants to combat that very skepticism. If we attribute irony to Socrates, he is not saying that no successful account can be given of reality but that the very idea of such an account is confused. Plato would believe Socrates is saying that we must be content with the various conceptions of reality to be found within our diverse activities. Plato would think this conclusion settles for the arbitrary, for the arts or activities we *happen* to have. The Sophists, on reflection, might settle for saying that discourse is a matter of skill in moving from art to art. But Plato wants to say that their position would be a denial of the reality of discourse. Discourse is more than a collection of arbitrary activities, and living is more than the skill of moving from one activity to the other. But what 'more' can discourse be, if we have already agreed that no measure of reality of the kind offered by the pre-Socratics is possible? That is Plato's big question.

Plato's answer, it could be argued, has two aspects. First, he emphasizes the importance of dialogue. Human activities cannot be treated as a collection of arbitrary arts. They stand in a dialogic relation to one another. When Socrates discusses the separate arts in Plato's *Gorgias,* he does not give a great deal of attention to their occurring in a discourse wider than themselves, although there is a suggestion to Callicles, at one point, that were it not for a common discourse, he and Callicles could not understand each other. Wittgenstein would say that it is the fact that we understand one another that constitutes our common discourse. Certainly, Socrates does not suggest that the reality of the arts, their being what they are, is internally related to discourse, to the ways in which we talk to one another, although he does insist, as against the Sophists, that there is something to understand, that each art has its logos.

But none of this is sufficient for Plato. He wants to go further by asking how we know that there *is* any reality in the different ways in which we talk to one another. For Plato, we have to show that these ways of talking themselves correspond to a Reality that is independent of them. This is what leads him to say that all discourse is about Reality. Plato never succeeds in giving a very clear account of how discourse *is* related to Reality, although he has much to say about accounts that must be rejected. He remains acutely aware of the problem of measuring the measure that would arise were he to give the kind of answer found in the pre-Socratics. But he is dangerously close to this problem when he suggests that all discourse has a common subject—namely, Reality. And yet he believed that philosophical authorship has to do with the investigation of that subject. This belief is what shows that he has a contemplative conception of philosophy. If, on the other hand, we are simply puzzled by the differences between human activities and want to clarify them, the big question or puzzle about the reality of discourse itself need not arise. That reality would simply be taken for granted in the concern with marking off different kinds of discourse. In relation to Wittgenstein, as we shall see later, it could be said that his philosophy would not be contemplative, in my sense, were we to think that all it amounted to was clarifying distinctions between language games. We would have omitted the fundamental questions which those distinctions subserve.

I have discussed the pre-Socratics, the Sophists, Socrates, and Plato because doing so helps me to formulate the problem which I want to pose in this opening chapter but which is also to be the theme of the book: How can one develop a contemplative conception of philosophy, given the difficulties we have mentioned? The problem of philosophical authorship, in the light of our discussion, may be summarized as follows:

(a) Philosophy is an attempt to give an account of Reality.

(b) If one provides any measure of 'the real', one can always, in turn, pose a question about the reality of the measure. No measure offered can avoid this difficulty.

(c) As a result of (b) one may abandon the whole enterprise of giving an account of reality and embrace a skepticism about any notion of reality.

(d) As a result of (b) one may admit that it makes sense to seek an account of reality but be entirely skeptical as to whether one can, in fact, arrive at an adequate account.

(e) As a result of (b) one may assume that philosophy cannot give an account of Reality as a whole, because that conception is confused. No one measure of 'the real' can be provided. What we need to recognize is that in human activities there are many conceptions of 'the real' and 'the unreal'. Philosophy must settle for pointing this out, clarifying the differences between them, and locating the confusion of attempting to transcend them in a more comprehensive account of Reality.

(f) Despite recognizing the difficulties mentioned in (b), philosophy's task described in (a) is not abandoned as it is in the different reactions found in (c), (d), and (e). All our discourse refers to Reality. Were that not so, our dialogues would simply be an absurd collection of arbitrary activities.

The question I will pursue is this: I, too, want to reject the reactions found in (c), (d) and (e), but I also reject the conclusions found in (f). I do not see how they can avoid the problem of measuring the measure mentioned in (b). What is the one Reality to which all discourse refers? Or, what is *the* relation in which all discourse stands to Reality? I accept that there are various distinctions between 'the real' and 'the unreal' in discourse and that they do not all have something in common; they are not subject to 'a common measure'. That is what is valuable in the reactions of (b) and (e). Yet I want to agree with (f) that if one settles for the differences emphasized in (e), one leaves out the fundamental questions in philosophy about the nature of reality. My question is,

How can philosophy give an account of reality which shows that it is necessary to go beyond simply noting differences between various modes of discourse, without invoking a common measure of 'the real' or assuming that all modes of discourse have a common subject, namely, Reality? Contemplative conceptions of philosophy engage with the question of the nature of reality, but come to very different conclusions. The contemplative conception of philosophy I shall be concerned with is one that attempts to answer the question I have posed. In this attempt it will be necessary, again and again, to show that I am not falling back into the attempt to give a single account of Reality. Thus much of the time I will emphasize the differences philosophy must respect by recognizing them. But those differences are not the end of the philosophical story. They can only be the differences they are because their reality depends on the place they occupy in human life. This is why Wittgenstein said that to imagine a language—discourse—is to imagine a way of living. The contemplative conception of philosophy I will talk about and, hopefully, express in my discussions is one that engages with the implications of Wittgenstein's remark, not least its implications for philosophical authorship.

2 Kierkegaard's Qualitative Dialectic

In the last chapter, I considered reactions to the recognition that philosophy cannot provide a common measure for 'the real'. If a philosophical author cannot give a substantive account of the nature of reality, can that authorship remain a serious one? The Sophists believed that it could not; Socrates thought that it could. If we read Socrates as saying, "There is no general account of reality; we must settle for the understanding that each art provides," this conclusion would not have satisfied Plato. As I have noted, he would want to know whether the arts themselves refer to reality. For Plato, it is not our practices that determine what we mean by reality but Reality that determines what we should say of our practices. Plato seems to seek a vantage point beyond all our practices, one that has been called "the view from Nowhere."[1] But what if, like the Sophists, and perhaps Socrates, we agree that such a vantage point is a fiction? What is the consequence for philosophical authorship?

In this chapter I will explore this question in relation to the pseudonymous works of Søren Kierkegaard. Because the twists and turns in the chapter are many, it may be helpful if I give, at the outset, a map of the terrain I will traverse.

I begin with an account of Kierkegaard's early worries about Socratic irony. At that time, he thought that an ironist is related playfully, and hence superficially, to the ways of living on which he comments. The ironist refuses to commit himself or herself to any of them. Kierkegaard holds that there is something treacherous in wanting to be a mere observer.

1. Thomas Nagel, *The View from Nowhere* (New York: Oxford University Press, 1986).

Second, I discuss Josiah Thompson's claim that the worries Kierke-gaard had about Socrates can be directed to Kierkegaard's relation to his pseudonymous works. Is not his attitude, too, one of a playful aes-thete? Does not Kierkegaard describe all his pseudonymous works as aesthetic?

Third, I reject attempts by James Conant to deflect Thompson's ac-cusations. Conant suggests that Thompson draws illegitimate conclu-sions about Kierkegaard's intellectual investigations on the basis of al-legations about Kierkegaard's private life, and that confuses 'lower' and 'higher' forms of 'the aesthetic'. I contend that Thompson *is* at-tacking Kierkegaard's methods, not his private life. Given the demise of foundationalism, Thompson questions the very possibility of philo-sophical inquiry. In short, he attacks 'the aesthetic' in an intellectual, that is, 'higher', sense.

Fourth, I discuss my disagreements with Conant about the nature of Kierkegaard's pseudonymous authorship. We both agree that Kierke-gaard is concerned with making grammatical distinctions in order to clarify the nature of religious belief. But Conant thinks that the pseu-donym Johannes Climacus ends up in self-contradiction and that Kier-kegaard, in his *Philosophical Fragments* and *Concluding Unscientific Post-script*, wrote works to show why the standpoints expressed in these works must be revoked. I do not accept this claim. A systematic philos-ophy, such as Hegel's, is certainly revoked, but is this true of the con-ceptual analysis by means of which this conclusion is reached?

Fifth, I argue that there is not a necessary tension between concep-tual analysis and religious belief. A tension arises only if one thinks that conceptual clarity is the same as the personal appropriation of reli-gious belief. Kierkegaard insists that there is an infinite distance be-tween them.

Finally, I claim that a contemplative conception of philosophy is not to be found in Kierkegaard. He is a religious thinker, concerned with specific confusions concerning Christianity. Kierkegaard never doubts the categories of the aesthetic, the ethical, and the religious, whereas Wittgenstein wonders at their very possibility. An asymmetry therefore exists between their authorships.

In his early doctoral dissertation, Kierkegaard shared Plato's misgiv-ings about Socrates' conception of philosophical authorship. If each art has its own *logos,* in what sense is the philosopher related to the arts?

Kierkegaard's fear is that he is related to them as a playful aesthete: elucidating them without being committed to any of them. For Kierkegaard, this is the 'infinite negativity' Socrates falls into by becoming the victim of his own irony: "The ironist stands proudly withdrawn into himself; he lets mankind pass before him, as did Adam the animals, and finds no companionship for himself.... For him life is a drama. He is himself a spectator even when performing some act.... He is inspired by the virtues of self-sacrifice as a spectator is inspired by them in a theatre." According to Kierkegaard, such an ironist "lives hypothetically and subjunctively, his life finally loses all continuity. With this he sinks completely into mood. His life becomes *sheer mood.*"[2]

Kierkegaard makes these remarks in a section called "irony after Fichte," but they also apply to Socrates. As Josiah Thompson has said, "In the last third of the book Kierkegaard turns from a consideration of Socratic irony to the concept of irony itself," but obviously, Socrates is not excluded from that wider context.[3] The subtitle of *The Concept of Irony* is *With Constant Reference to Socrates* (Capel translation) or *With Continual Reference to Socrates* (Hong translation). It is also true that, in this section, Kierkegaard speaks of the romanticist rather than the ironist. The romanticist is someone who lives poetically, feeling free to pick up or drop perspectives in the imagination, without being committed to any of them. This cannot be said of Socrates. The point is that at this early stage in his views, Kierkegaard thought that it could. This is the Kierkegaard who writes: "Throughout this discussion I use the expressions *irony* and *ironist,* but I could as easily say: *romanticism* and *romanticist.* Both expressions designate the same thing."[4] Kierkegaard's challenge seems to be this: if philosophy cannot show us which of our practices refer to Reality or if it cannot show that they all have

2. Søren Kierkegaard, *The Concept of Irony, with Constant Reference to Socrates,* trans. with an introduction by Lee M. Capel (London: Collins, 1966), pp. 300–302.
3. Josiah Thompson, *Kierkegaard* (London: Gollancz, 1978), p. 148.
4. Kierkegaard, *Concept of Irony,* p. 292. Connections between the demise of philosophy's traditional task of discovering the nature of reality and romanticism continue to be drawn. I heard Richard Rorty in a discussion at Claremont say that given this demise, we are called to live as creative romantics, creating meanings for our lives. We are bidden to be poets. The trouble, according to Rorty, is that having to work as they do, few have sufficient leisure for the task. On the other hand, Stanley Cavell, according to Stephen Mulhall, has taken romanticism's conception of a world-creating and self-creating genius "and simply universalised or democratised it by attributing the capacity for such reanimation to anyone possessed of language" (Stephen Mulhall, *Stanley Cavell: Philosophy's Recounting of the Ordinary* [Oxford: Clarendon Press, 1994], p. 166). I do not approve of

their place in a comprehensive metaphysical system that shows the structure of Reality, how can it be related to these practices in anything other than an aesthetic way? The seriousness of this charge is brought home to us if we remember Kierkegaard's depiction of an aesthete in his *Either/Or*:

> One is struck by seeing a clown whose joints are so limber that all necessity for maintaining the human gait and posture is done away. Such are you in an intellectual sense, you can just as well stand on your head as on your feet, everything is possible for you, and by this possibility you can astonish others and yourself; but it is unwholesome, and for the sake of your own tranquillity I beg you to see to it that what is your advantage, does not end up by being a curse. A man who has a conviction cannot turn topsy-turvy upon himself and all things. I warn you, therefore, not against the world but against yourself, and I warn the world against you.[5]

Commenting on this depiction, Conant says:

> Thus, the work portrays a character who is an aesthete by providing the reader with a view of such a life from the inside. The implied author of the work is someone whose life consists of playing with possibilities: imaginatively taking up perspectives, assuming the part of different characters and thereby temporarily occupying the roles of a variety of personae, and under such pretences vicariously or tentatively entering into experiences or relationships in order to be able to savour certain pleasures, emotions or moods.... [W]e might say that the defining feature of an ethical individual—that which he possesses and the aesthete lacks—is *character.* For the aesthete's life, as depicted, is devoid of all the exercises through which character is fashioned.... Kierkegaard elsewhere ... suggests that there is a sense in which what the thoroughgoing aesthete lacks is a *self.* Such a vicariously lived existence consists in a systematic evasion of those moments through which a self is articulated.[6]

If, therefore, we claim that to be a philosophical author is to be an aesthete, the author is accused of simply playing with possibilities in his or

---

these recourses to romanticism. I certainly do not think they are underwritten by philosophy.

5. Søren Kierkegaard, *Either/Or,* trans. Walter Lowrie, vol. 2 (London: Oxford University Press, 1946), p. 14.

6. James Conant, "Putting Two and Two Together: Kierkegaard, Wittgenstein, and the Point of View for Their Work as Authors," in *Philosophy and the Grammar of Religious Belief,* ed. Timothy Tessin and Mario von der Ruhr (London: Macmillan; New York: St. Martin's Press, 1995), p. 254.

her work, work that has no character. In his or her work, on this view, a philosopher lives vicariously, entering imaginatively, but not really, into the possibilities and perspectives depicted.

But if Kierkegaard had these worries about Socrates, Thompson had comparable worries about Kierkegaard. These worries centered on the qualitative dialectic exemplified in his pseudonymous works, in which Kierkegaard explores various perspectives from the inside. But how is he himself related to them? Thompson replies that Kierkegaard's "pseudonyms testify to the activity of a powerful aesthete, withdrawn from the actualities of life, which is all philosophy can be once its metaphysical pretensions have been put aside." His conclusion is that in the pseudonymous works "there is an underlying black humour. For finally the joke is on the reader, and the smarter he is, the sooner he realises it. But to see through all the pseudonyms, to recognise that the vision of any one of them is not to be preferred to any other, is finally to join Kierkegaard in his cloister. It is to share with him that peculiarly modern laceration—'I must believe, but I can't believe'— which since his time has become even more painful."[7]

Thompson is denying *the very possibility of authentic authorship in philosophy* after the demise of metaphysics. His challenge deserves serious attention; it cannot be brushed aside. It does not depend on biographical claims about Kierkegaard. Thompson is not arguing that Kierkegaard is an aesthete in his work because he is an aesthete in his private life. But Conant thinks otherwise, positing that such inquiries become "enmeshed in a biographical dispute about what we can conclude about Kierkegaard the author."[8]

Even if this were the basis of Thompson's challenge, it cannot be disposed of as summarily as Conant suggests. He asks: "How damning is this charge? Even if one were to grant it, might one not reply: if the author has succeeded in imparting to me an insight into the unsatisfactoriness of the purely aesthetic mode of life, then, even if he has failed to act on this insight himself, that in no way invalidates the genuineness of the insight he imparts. He may be a fool or a hypocrite, but that does not give me a reason to be one as well." Kierkegaard, through depicting aesthetic and ethical perspectives in his pseudonymous

7. Thompson, *Kierkegaard,* pp. 202, 147.
8. Conant, "Putting Two and Two Together," p. 256.

works, hopes to jolt his readers into a realization that they are not leading a Christian life. But, Conant argues, "it does not follow that the efficacy or the genuineness of the confrontations which the work wishes to so arrange therefore ultimately hinges upon a relation that Kierkegaard's own life bears to a mode of life depicted within the pseudonymous authorship."[9]

As a *general* thesis, the complete insulation of the efficacy of a work from the life of an author cannot be sustained. The force of the thesis has to do with an understandable resistance to the lamentable practice of dragging extraneous features from authors' lives into the interpretation of their works. But when this becomes a general thesis, it falls foul of counterexamples. Rush Rhees told me of a poet who was thought to write fine, patriotic verse. It turned out that throughout the time he was doing so, he had been a quisling. It was impossible to read his poems in the same way again. According to the general thesis, we should be able to say that the fine patriotic verse is not vitiated by the facts about his character. Its effect should be the same despite the hypocrisy of the poet. But this is what proved to be impossible: the lines mocked the reader. If Thompson were simply accusing Kierkegaard of hypocrisy, then, contra Conant, finding it established might have a similar effect. The joke would be on us, and the pseudonymous works might mock us with their playfulness.

Nevertheless, the discussion of the relation between a philosopher's work and her or his private life takes us away from the central issue: How is philosophical authorship, as such, taken up into a life? If there were a strict demarcation between an author's work and his or her life, we should be able to say with Andrey Sinyavsky, "You may live like a fool and yet have excellent ideas from time to time."[10] But can we say, "You may live like a fool and be engaged in serious philosophical inquiry"?

Part of the difficulty is to avoid a silly moralism in this connection. Suppose we say that a philosophical life is worth living. This does not mean that there is something independent of philosophy by appeal to which this worth can be established. There is an internal relation between the worth and the inquiry.

9. Ibid., pp. 255, 257.
10. Andrey Sinyavsky, *Unguarded Thoughts* (London: Collins and Harvill Press, 1965), p. 7.

In a television interview, I tried to make a distinction between struggling with conceptual issues about worship and struggling to worship. My interviewer suggested that to do so leads to a kind of schizophrenia, a suspect separation between D. Z. Phillips as a philosopher and D. Z. Phillips as a person. The suggestion was a kind of accusation meant to create guilt at the thought that unless philosophy *is* taken up into one's life, it cannot be more than a trivial, marginal pursuit.

'Taken up into one's life', in the interviewer's sense, meant something like the moral and religious benefits of philosophizing on one's own life and the lives of others. The benefits, so conceived, are independent of philosophy and intelligible independent of it. But we are close to the pharisaical suggestion that a moral philosopher should be better than other people and that a philosopher of religion is someone who knows more about God than do other people. It is partly to avoid such suggestions that Rush Rhees says: "Above all one must avoid the suggestion that 'the philosophical life' is the kind of life you must lead *if* you are to do philosophy: as if doing philosophy and leading the kind of life were distinct or separable. As though it made *sense* to say, 'It is a pity that you cannot do philosophy without going the hard way—or it is a pity that you cannot do philosophy and also lead a life of self-indulgence—but I am afraid there is no other way'. As though the checking of self-indulgence were the *price* that you have to pay in order to be able to do philosophy. All this is nonsense: but it is not easy to make *this* clear."[11]

By contrast, Rhees emphasizes the kind of *attention* philosophy asks of one. Giving *that* kind of attention to certain problems *is* the philosophical life, and that attention is not easily acquired. According to Rhees: "This is what Wittgenstein implies when he says that in philosophy one has to struggle constantly against a resistance within oneself, which is a resistance of *will*. One is unwilling to let certain ways of thinking go. It was in such connexions also that Wittgenstein said that whoever does philosophy will have to *suffer*." Is not this also why Rhees says, "We may feel that there is something more like an internal connexion between what you are engaged on in philosophy, and the sort of life you lead"?[12] But that "internal connexion" comes about through

11. Rush Rhees, "The Fundamental Problems of Philosophy," ed. Timothy Tessin, *Philosophical Investigations* 17, 4 (October 1994): 577.
12. Ibid.

the kind of attention philosophy demands of one. This is not to deny that there may be occasions in a person's life when the difficulties faced are both moral and philosophical. Or one might not want to make any distinction. But if one wanted to show the *distinctive* way in which philosophy can be taken up in a person's life, one would not choose *those* examples. This is why Rhees states that "in a sense it is stupid to ask or to speak of *why* philosophy is important. The danger is of confusion in the conception of what you 'get out of it.' The danger of giving attention to what is happening to me, or what is happening to the pupil, and being distracted from attention to what is being discussed, or to the questions that had been asked and are being investigated."[13]

If we now look back at Thompson's skeptical challenge to philosophy, we can see that it is far more serious than one might suppose at first. Thompson is not simply attacking someone he takes to be a hypocritical philosopher. If *that* is what he were doing, we could reply by saying that not all philosophers are hypocritical. Thompson is challenging *the very possibility* of philosophy once one admits that it cannot discover the nature and essence of reality. Once that task is abandoned, investigation degenerates into the ephemeral interests of the aesthete. Thompson establishes this conclusion *not* by reference to Kierkegaard's private life but by reference to the nature of his pseudonymous works.

What makes it difficult to embrace this conclusion is that Thompson does draw on two major incidents in Kierkegaard's life. His purpose in doing so, however, is not to find *external* evidence in Kierkegaard's life for what he finds in his work but to illustrate *the same aesthetic tendencies* that he finds in the pseudonymous works.

The first incident comes from Kierkegaard's childhood. His father had promised to take him for a walk, but it had become too late to fulfil the promise. Instead, the young boy was taken on an imaginary walk by his father in the drawing room. Kierkegaard complained, later, that much of his childhood had been lived in the imagination. Thompson, as we have seen, suggests that Kierkegaard, in his pseudonymous works, is playing with possibilities. In referring to the childhood incident, Thompson is showing that this form of play—that is, the *same* form of play—developed early in Kierkegaard. Thompson is providing

13. Ibid., p. 582.

not a confirmation but an early illustration of the imaginative play he finds in the pseudonymous works. That is why there is a continuity in the "singular thought" that appears early and late in Kierkegaard: "Slowly, inevitably, a singular thought has taken root in the young boy's mind. It is not necessary to live in the world. On the contrary, the world—its resistance, its burdens, its conflicting demands—can be transformed. One need only dream. Narcissus has found his solitary pool and Kierkegaard his future: he will be a dreamer."[14] Thompson is not confirming Kierkegaard's vocation by an appeal to something external to it; rather, he is claiming to have located *the birth of that vocation,* in Kierkegaard's childhood. His general claim is that philosophers bereft of a metaphysical vision are fated to become idle dreamers.

The second incident Thompson refers to concerns Kierkegaard's reaction on hearing a poorhouse inmate bewail her want of a certain sum of money. Kierkegaard provided the exact sum with a flourish before vanishing. Later, in tranquillity, he indulged in ruminating on the different ways in which the poor woman might have thought of the incident. Thompson's claim is that in these ruminations we have the *same* tendency to live poetically in the imagination that he finds in the pseudonymous works.

Thompson's charge is general and extensive, since he notes that Kierkegaard calls all his pseudonymous works aesthetic. But given Kierkegaard's unflattering depiction of the aesthete, how can any work called 'aesthetic' enjoy intellectual respectability? *That* is the core of Thompson's challenge.

This challenge is not easily deflected. It cannot be achieved, as Conant thinks, simply by not indulging in what he calls "flattening out the category of the aesthetic."[15] Conant's proposed solution simply postpones really facing Thompson's challenge. Conant argues that the category of the aesthetic is flattened out when 'the aesthetic' is equated with 'immediacy'. Within the three categories of 'the religious', 'the ethical', and 'the aesthetic', there are higher and lower levels. Conant endeavors to show what this distinction comes to within the aesthetic category: "The most primitive stage of the aesthetic is, indeed, that of 'immediacy.' In immediacy there is a complete absorption of the self in the object.... At this lowest (and, in a sense, purest) stage of the aesthetic, the accent falls totally on the object; the subject plays a purely

14. Thompson, *Kierkegaard,* p. 40.
15. Conant, "Putting Two and Two Together," p. 309 n. 32.

nominal, spectorial role." But if, as Conant notes, the most pure form of the aesthetic is that which is "available to a pre-linguistic infant," the account, rather than falling on the object, falls entirely on the self.[16] This is the kind of immediacy where desire finds its elemental gratification in the organism in which it originates. What of the higher levels? Conant argues:

> What has been lost on a great deal of the secondary literature, however, is that this stage (of immediate absorption) does not exhaust the category of the aesthetic; it is only one stage of the aesthetic. In the 'higher' stages of the aesthetic, in which the subject takes up a more reflective attitude towards the object, there is a sense in which the relation (between subject and object) at issue for Kierkegaard still remains a purely contemplative one.... The critical feature that the different stages of the aesthetic have in common is that (as Kierkegaard likes to put it) the accent falls on the object rather than the subject—it is a relation that makes no demands on the subject's mode of existence.... The point of grouping complete immediacy and certain forms of mediation (i.e. forms of 'disinterested reflectiveness') together within a single category is to highlight their common feature: in each case, the subject's attention is directed away from itself and towards the object of its attention.[17]

Conant's suggestion that the most indulgent aesthete and the most serious, disinterested inquirer should be placed within the single category of the aesthetic because they share a common feature is reminiscent of John Stuart Mill's attempt to contain radically different activities within the category of 'pleasure' by introducing the distinction between higher and lower pleasures. The difficulty for this philosophical strategy is well known: it is not the alleged common category that gives sense to the activities but the activities that give sense to the concepts connected with them. It is not the category of pleasure that throws light on the activities in which we speak of pleasure but the activities which give sense to the assertion that they give us pleasure. Similarly, it is not the category of the aesthetic that illuminates the activity but the activity that shows why we can speak of the aesthetic in connection with it. The qualitative differences are, at the same time, grammatical differences, and these cannot be bypassed by an appeal to an alleged common feature they all share. To place delight in Joe's ice cream and grappling with one's philosophical puzzlement within the

16. Ibid.
17. Ibid., p. 309 n. 32.

category of the aesthetic, on the grounds that to do so highlights a common feature they share—the way a "subject's attention is directed away from itself and towards the object of its attention"—does not seem to be a step toward grammatical enlightenment. The *differences* between the examples are infinitely more important than the supposed common feature invoked, as in Mill's case, to hold a suspect category intact.

Conant states that "Kierkegaard refers to the entire pseudonymous authorship as an aesthetic production. He insists therefore upon the very fact that Thompson wants to surprise him with: namely, that Kierkegaard's own relation to the content of these works is in a sense a merely aesthetic one—it is that of a poetic or literary author to his poetic or literary creations."[18] But before we can conclude that Kierkegaard and Thompson are referring to the very same fact, the same aesthetic relation, we have to ask how each of them understands that aesthetic relation. Once we do so, we see why Conant's distinction between higher and lower levels of the aesthetic does not meet Thompson's challenge.

Thompson's problem is to see how Kierkegaard can call his pseudonymous works 'aesthetic', at the same time as Kierkegaard conducts a blistering attack on the attitude of the aesthete. Conant seeks to reassure us that the attitude attacked belongs to the lower levels of the aesthetic, whereas Kiekegaard's aesthetic belongs to its higher levels. But when we remind ourselves that the lower levels, according to Conant, have to do with immediacy, with the gratifications of a prelinguistic infant, it is clear that the imaginative play of the young Kierkegaard and, even more, Kierkegaard's poetic reflections on the woman from the poorhouse belong to what Conant calls the higher levels of the aesthetic. Further, as we have seen, Thompson sees these examples as the birth and an example, respectively, of the *same form* of poetic play he takes Kierkegaard's pseudonymous works to be. So Thompson's worry about the nature of philosophical inquiry surfaces *within* the higher levels of the aesthetic.

In addition, it is clear that Kierkegaard himself recognizes the dangers of aestheticism *in the realm of the intellect;* in *Either/Or,* as we have seen, he speaks of the readiness, intellectually, to stand on one's head

---

18. Ibid., p. 258.

as easily as on one's feet, to turn topsy-turvy on any question. No reminder of the lower levels of the aesthetic can deflect a charge of corruption of the intellect. Thompson's challenge is to show why such corruption is not *inevitable* if philosophers pretend that their inquiries can continue, even *after* they admit that they are not discovering the nature of reality. What else can philosophy be but an empty aestheticism?

Conant wants to argue that we may think such conclusions face us only if we ignore the sense in which Kierkegaard's pseudonymous works are 'aesthetic'. Conant's suggestion is, in certain ways, similar to some views of Socrates that we considered in the last chapter. Socrates brought people to see, indirectly, that it makes no sense to seek a conception of reality that transcends our practices. Kierkegaard, like Socrates, is telling us to be content with clarity about the practices we engage in. An aesthetic interest is a disinterestedness in becoming clear about the practices. Thus, if we give proper understanding to the pseudonymous works, we shall come to a fruitful postmetaphysical understanding of philosophical authorship.

There are two observations to be made about these conclusions. First, if this is how Kierkegaard's authorship is to be understood, no contemplative conception of philosophy is to be found in his work, because we can be puzzled about differences between our practices, our modes of discourse, without being puzzled about how discourse is at all possible—the puzzle that is the hallmark of a contemplative conception of philosophy.

Second, even allowing that the philosophy one finds in Kierkegaard has to do with conceptual clarifications in a noncontemplative sense, those clarifications have their place in an authorship that is primarily religious rather than philosophical. But these observations must now be substantiated.

Conant argues that the pseudonymous works are written to be revoked. A systematic point of view is elucidated in such a way that we come to appreciate the confusion involved in it. The pseudonymous works invite us to explore them, but in the course of doing so, we come to see why they must be abandoned. Through the abandonment we achieve conceptual clarification.

Conceptual clarification is an activity that is not easy to understand. It is *essentially indirect*. What it achieves is not the refutation of a false thesis but the unraveling of a confusion. A confused statement is not refuted, for its refutation would involve thinking of it as intelligible, but false; the trouble consists in the fact that an attempt is made to say what does not make sense. The route to the confusion has to be unfolded in such a way that the person no longer wants to utter it. The unfolding is indirect in that one has to begin from where the confused one is.

Kierkegaard had particular confusions in mind. He called them 'the monstrous illusion', by which he meant the pervasive illusion in the Denmark of his day that led people to think they were Christians when they were not. If we accept that Kierkegaard's conceptual clarifications were occasioned by his concern about 'the monstrous illusion', his conception of philosophy in such clarifications is obvious: it is an underlaborer conception of philosophy.

Locke thought that system building was the province of science. In attempting to build metaphysical systems, philosophy was the trespasser. That being so, what task remains for philosophy? Locke's view was that a useful but more modest task awaits it—namely, to be an underlaborer on the sites on which others build and live. Philosophy clears away conceptual confusions to facilitate clear building and clear living. Conceptual underlaborers clear up conceptual confusions on one site after another. If we ask underlaborers where their *own* site is, the question betrays our misunderstanding. It does not make sense to attribute a site to them; their work is occasioned by confusions that occur on *other* sites. Philosophy has no distinctive site of its own, and that is why, on this view, we always have to speak of the philosophy *of* something or other—philosophy of morals, philosophy of psychology, philosophy of religion, and so on.

Kierkegaard's main concern is with confusions about religion. In exploring them, he brings many conceptual distinctions to our attention. We can call them philosophical distinctions if we want to, but Kierkegaard's interest in making them is not primarily philosophical. He is, above all, a religious thinker, which is why, I argue, we do not find a contemplative conception of philosophy in his work. Conant does not see this point because for him, too, philosophy is primarily a matter of clarifying conceptual confusions. The point could be expressed by saying that, as far as the *character* of the inquiry is concerned, Conant settles for Kierkegaard's qualitative dialectic.

Kierkegaard's religious purposes are evident when he writes: "Supposing that ... a reader understands perfectly and appraises critically the individual aesthetic productions, he will nevertheless totally misunderstand me, inasmuch as he does not understand the religious totality in my whole work as an author. Suppose, then, another understands my works in the totality of their religious reference, but does not understand a single one of the aesthetic productions contained in them—I would say that the lack of understanding is not an essential lack."[19]

I had written, "What needs to be emphasised is that Kierkegaard is not simply clearing up grammatical confusions but, in depicting aesthetic, ethical and religious perspectives, challenging people about the meaning of their own lives."[20] Conant responds, "Phillips gets into a muddle of trying to distinguish Kierkegaard from Wittgenstein." He thinks I make this attempt because of a "misplaced worry: 'The question is how much of what Kierkegaard describes as the illusion is to be described as grammatical?' The correct answer which Phillips feels he must reject is: 100 per cent."[21]

At first it seems that Conant is forming a clear distinction between making grammatical observations and the philosophical or religious purposes for which they are made. But then he says, "That does not mean that Kierkegaard *merely* wishes to draw attention to a confusion of grammar." We now have a distinction between 'drawing attention to a confusion of grammar' and 'merely drawing attention to a confusion of grammar', which presumably Conant takes to be a distinction of substance. But then it turns out, according to Conant, that to talk of 'merely drawing attention to a confusion of grammar' is *itself* a confusion of grammar: the confusion of not realizing that drawing attention to a confusion of grammar "*in the relevant sense* is not merely about words."[22]

I have italicized "in the relevant sense" because Conant, like myself, wants to emphasize the internal relations in Kierkegaard between "drawing attention to a confusion of grammar" and his concern with 'the monstrous illusion'. Conant says that it is a *confusion* to talk of "confusions of grammar" in Kierkegaard "as if this were somehow distinct from a confusion in how his purportedly 'Christian' readership lives. Such confusions of grammar are not mere confusions of gram-

---

19. Søren Kierkegaard, *The Point of View for My Work as an Author,* trans. Walter Lowrie (Oxford: Oxford University Press, 1939), p. 6.
20. D. Z. Phillips, "Authorship and Authenticity: Kierkegaard and Wittgenstein," in *Wittgenstein and Religion* (London: Macmillan; New York: St. Martin's Press, 1993), p. 211.
21. Conant, "Putting Two and Two Together," p. 281.
22. Ibid.

mar (because grammar in the relevant sense is not merely about words), but also confusion in life. They are symptoms (and sometimes contributory causes) of soul-sickness." By contrast, Conant thinks that I have missed the internal relation between Kierkegaard's conceptual clarifications and his concern with 'the monstrous illusion' and that I treat them as two separate matters: "Phillips is misled by Bouwsma into thinking that part of the illusion has to do with a grammatical issue and then a separate part of the illusion has to do with a religious issue. But the only real issue that the pseudonymous authorship wants to raise for its reader is simultaneously a grammatical (or, in Kierkegaard's parlance, 'dialectical') one: namely, the fact that an examination of the reader's life will reveal that it is not one in which, as it is presently constituted, a religious issue can find a foothold. The 'monstrous illusion' is therefore at bottom a grammatical one."[23] But, presumably, it is not *merely* a grammatical one if Conant wants to retain his previous distinctions.

As we shall see in the next chapter, part of the trouble comes from Conant's desire to find too tidy a parallel between Kierkegaard and Wittgenstein. In fact, there is an important asymmetry between Kierkegaard's qualitative dialectic and Wittgenstein's philosophical method. For the moment, however, we can begin to approach these issues by showing why a contemplative conception of philosophy is absent in Kierkegaard's work.

As we have seen, Conant attributes to me a "two-part" view of grammatical confusion in Kierkegaard's inquiries: "Phillips's way of posing the issue makes it seem as if, in the pseudonymous works, Kierkegaard is doing two separate things: (1) clearing up certain grammatical confusions, (2) challenging his readers to examine their lives. And so now it can seem as if there is an asymmetry between Kierkegaard and Wittgenstein: Wittgenstein does the first of these things but not the second."[24] According to Conant, I think the second issue involves a desire in Kierkegaard to push people in the direction of Christianity and that in so doing I share in the widespread misunderstanding of Kierkegaard's pseudonymous works in the secondary literature.

23. Ibid.
24. Ibid., pp. 279–80.

Conant gives a good account of the aim of a pseudonymous work: "The sense in which Kierkegaard understands his purpose in the aesthetic works to be a religious one has to do with the task of clearing up confusions about what sort of life a religious life is (and thereby clearing certain obstacles from the path of his readers if they wish to embark on such a life). The aim of the authorship is to mark out the path of such a life more clearly. That is the most a religious author can do. If the authorship were successful in its aim, what this would mean with respect to the majority of his readers is simply that they would no longer pretend that they are Christians."[25]

Rather than say that the purpose of the pseudonymous works is to push people toward Christianity, all I said was that it is Kierkegaard's concern about Christianity which leads him to make the qualitative distinctions that he does. It is important to recognize that this concern gives Kierkegaard's qualitative dialectic its rationale. I had stated: "Kierkegaard's hope was that when aesthetic and ethical perspectives are seen for what they are, those who confused them with Christianity would realise the error of their ways and turn to Christianity. But even if this does not happen, and they preferred to stay where they were, at least the monstrous illusion would have been dispelled. 'Therefore it is possible for misunderstanding to be removed and become agreement and understanding, but it is possible also for it to be removed and to become real disagreement.' It follows that clarity is in 'every man's interest, whether he be a Christian or not, whether his intention is to accept Christianity or to reject it.'"[26]

So at no time did I suggest that Kierkegaard's qualitative dialectic, of itself, pushes people toward Christianity. I said, explicitly, "It would be problematic to argue that Kierkegaard thought ... that philosophical reflection, if carried out with integrity, should lead one to see Christianity as the only adequate positive answer to the question of the meaning of life."[27]

What I want to emphasize, again and again, is that Kierkegaard's qualitative dialectic gets its purpose, its point, and its character from his religious concern. As Conant recognizes, it is in this context that Kierkegaard wants to deliver people from a confusion of categories:

25. Ibid., p. 279.
26. Phillips, "Authorship and Authenticity," pp. 205–6.
27. Ibid., p. 212.

"But the very specific grammatical confusions to which Kierkegaard wishes to draw attention are ones that only come into focus for the reader through an examination of his own life—through the realisation that religious categories do not have the weight in his life which he fantasises they do. The confusion cannot come into view for the reader unless he is brought to challenge himself about how he lives." So vital is this concern for Kierkegaard that, as Conant says, he would prefer the demise of Christianity to the triumph of 'the monstrous illusion': "Even if the effect of Kierkegaard's authorship were only to completely purge Denmark of all the people who wished to think of themselves as Christians, that would still constitute a significant advance. For it would clear the path for someone someday who did wish to become a Christian. In particular, it would allow it to once again become clear that a Christian is not something one simply is, but rather someone one must become: 'There is really something tragically true in the fact that it would be better if Christianity were not proclaimed at all than that it be done as it is now.... [T]he disaster is that people get used to hearing everything, without having the remotest notion of doing something.' "[28]

The internal relation between Kierkegaard's qualitative dialectic and his religious concern about 'the monstrous illusion' could not be put more bluntly than when Conant says, "If someone is not confused about the categories and does not pretend to be a Christian then he is not part of the monstrosity."[29] And to emerge from the illusion has its point in an *affective* relation in which the unconfused person stands to Christianity. Climacus, in the *Postscript*, puts it thus: "Christianity is subjectivity, an inner transformation, an actualization of inwardness, and ... only two kinds of people know anything about it: those who with an infinite passionate interest in an eternal happiness base their happiness upon their believing relationship to Christianity, and those who with an infinite passion, but in passion, reject it—the happy and the unhappy lovers."[30]

At no time does Kierkegaard doubt the categories of the aesthetic, the ethical, and the religious. His concern is with confusions between them. His qualitative dialectic is meant to bring out these confusions.

28. Conant, "Putting Two and Two Together," pp. 280, 325 n. 76.
29. Ibid., p. 321 n. 66.
30. Søren Kierkegaard, *Concluding Unscientific Postscript*, trans. David Swenson and Walter Lowrie (Princeton: Princeton University Press, 1944), p. 51.

As I have said, the conceptual distinctions made in the course of these clarifications may be called philosophical. Yet there is a problem in giving the dialectic overall a philosophical character, for philosophy itself is simply one subject within it.

Climacus, the pseudonymous author, is a philosopher who is not a Christian. Nevertheless, he is portrayed as having an interest in Christianity. So Kierkegaard, a religious author, creates Climacus, a philosophical author. At the end of his *Concluding Unscientific Postscript*, Climacus, in an appendix, tells us that the work is to be revoked. But in what sense? *That* is the vital question as far as Kierkegaard's relation to philosophical authorship is concerned. My view is that Kierkegaard the religious author makes Climacus the philosopher, who is not a Christian, tell us that his work is to be revoked, put aside, because it cannot answer a *religious* question: "I, Johannes Climacus, now thirty years of age, born in Copenhagen, a plain man like the common run of them, have heard tell of a highest good in prospect, which is called an eternal blessedness, and that Christianity will bestow this upon me on condition of adhering to it—now I ask how I am to become a Christian."[31]

Conant thinks that we are brought to see that the work must be revoked *philosophically*. He claims that it ends up in self-defeating confusions and contradictions. But viewed philosophically, this simply does not happen; rather, the work provides philosophical insights about the grammar of religious belief that are similar to those which Wittgenstein provides, which is not surprising given Kierkegaard's influence on Wittgenstein. But because Kierkegaard's primary interests are religious, Climacus's philosophical insights are brought into a final relation with what they cannot do—namely, make one embark on becoming a Christian. In his qualitative dialectic, Kierkegaard, because of his religious interest, gives pride of place to what philosophy *cannot* do. He does not give pride of place, as Wittgenstein does, to what philosophy *can* do. This is why we have to conclude that a contemplative conception of philosophy is not to be found in Kierkegaard.

The path to this conclusion is a complicated one, because Kierkegaard's pseudonymous authors create their own pseudonymous authors and pursue their own objects of criticism. Climacus, a philosopher, who is not a Christian, criticizes philosophical hubris with respect to Christianity. The main object of criticism, in this respect, is Hegel's

31. Ibid., p. 545.

System, the example, *par excellence,* of metaphysical ambition. Kierkegaard joked about how fortunate Hegel was to have been born late enough to see Reality reach its culmination in his own System! The System provides a higher form of understanding that transcends Christianity. Yet, it cannot be said, so far, that Climacus is critical of *any* form of philosophy, given that he himself is a philosopher and that his criticisms of Hegel's System are themselves philosophical.

But the plot thickens, since in the course of these criticisms, Climacus comes to conclusions which refer to philosophical tendencies with respect to religion that are far more extensive than Hegelianism. Climacus distinguishes between objective problems and subjective problems with respect to Christianity. "The objective problem consists of an inquiry into the truth of Christianity. The subjective problem concerns the relationship of the individual to Christianity. To put it quite simply: How may I, Johannes Climacus, participate in the happiness promised by Christianity?"[32] Climacus brings out the confusion of treating the subjective problem as though it were an objective one. This confusion is philosophy's main contribution to 'the monstrous illusion'. Although this is Climacus's philosophical view, according to Conant, it is one with which Kierkegaard agrees. Conant brings out well the kind of confusion attributed to philosophy:

> His view is that whenever modern philosophy tries to speak to the question of what it is to be a Christian, it unwittingly transforms a religious problem into an intellectual (i.e. epistemic or metaphysical) problem (a problem concerning, say, the sort of evidence upon which one should base one's belief, or how exactly one should best conceive of the difference between the divine and the human). Modern philosophy is, Kierkegaard thinks, thereby constantly mistaking something which properly belongs to the category of the aesthetic (a problem which can be approached through detached reflection) for something which belongs to the category of the religious (a problem which can only be encountered in the context of certain ways of acting).[33]

The plot thickens further. Climacus criticizes not only Hegel's System but also other tendencies that confuse religious and aesthetic categories. But these criticisms are themselves philosophical and are, therefore, in Kierkegaard's terms, aesthetic. But Conant wants to say that

---

32. Ibid., p. 20.
33. Conant, "Putting Two and Two Together," p. 261.

these philosophical criticisms, in turn, end up in confusion and contradiction. He argues that they involve a metaphysical view which Climacus himself has seen through. How can Conant say this? He does so
by changing a conceptual (or grammatical) observation made by Climacus into a philosophical thesis. In short, Conant becomes an illustration of the kind of contribution which Kierkegaard says that modern philosophy makes to 'the monstrous illusion'.

Climacus points out that within Christianity there is talk of a renunciation of the understanding. He is reminding us of a religious conception. An example would be the way in which Job renounces the understanding offered to him by his Comforters. Such a renunciation is
expressed further in his ability to say, "The Lord gave, the Lord hath
taken away. Blessed be the name of the Lord." Philosophy or philosophically informed theologies ignore this notion of renunciation in
the construction of theodicies.

When a philosopher provides this reminder in the way Climacus
does, he or she is not laying claim to a 'higher understanding' that
transcends Christianity but, rather, making a grammatical observation
about religious belief. But Conant turns Climacus's insight into a metaphysical theory: "This plea within the body of the book on behalf of a
renunciation of the understanding comes in the form of a doctrine as
to the true nature of Christianity, thus in the form of 'higher understanding.' We are invited to think that we can get a glimpse into the nature of something which the human understanding is unable to grasp."
On such a reading, all Conant can see here is "a self-defeating attempt
to penetrate the incomprehensible by trying to smuggle in a glimmer
of comprehension." As a result, "The *Postscript* begins as an attempt to
distinguish between 'subjective' and 'objective' problems.... But it comes
to seem as if this task of demarcation presupposes the existence of a
category of problem that reason cannot penetrate; it seems as if we
need to mark out that which reason can comprehend from that which
it cannot."[34]

Here, Conant has equated "a renunciation of the understanding"
of which Christianity talks in *specific* religious contexts with a general
metaphysical theory, hence the ready comparison with the *Tractatus:*

> The *Tractatus* begins as an attempt to clarify the logical structure of lan-
> guage. But this seems to presuppose that we be able to draw a limit to

34. Ibid., pp. 291, 292.

thought—to mark out those thoughts that can be accommodated by the logical structure of language from those that cannot. Both works thereby invite the reader to enter into a perspective from which it seems that there is something that reason *cannot* do.... Yet it also comes to seem as if the very philosophical exercise of identifying the limits of thought itself imparts to us a glimmer of comprehension into that which is incomprehensible; itself, it shows us the truth of thoughts which are logically unthinkable and hence incapable of being coherently stated.[35]

But, as H. A. Nielsen has shown, "The Unknown of the *Fragments* should not be run together with *epistemological* unknowns or unknowables such as Kant's Ding-an-sich or the Unknowable in Herbert Spencer's *First Principles*."[36] Nielsen's insight needs to be applied to the *Postscript* too. Commenting on Nielsen, I said:

> If we want to know what it means to speak of human inadequacy before God, we must examine, not epistemological theories, but how such talk enters the believer's life. Further, if we were trying to convey the sense of such a notion to a would-be believer "it would be beside the point to offer him a proof that some generalized or metaphysical limit of thought exists, such as 'the mystical' or 'the unsayable' in Wittgenstein's *Tractatus Logico-Philosophicus*." Climacus says categorically that God cannot be known by metaphysical proofs. To think otherwise, he claims, is to be in the grip of conceptual confusion. Yet "at the same time he speaks *knowingly* of this Unknown in expressions drawn from everyday religious language." Climacus, it seems, is trying to clarify what it means to talk of an Unknown God by placing such talk in its natural setting.[37]

Yet, even if I could persuade Conant of *this* conclusion, so wedded is he to his thesis that the *Postscript* must end in some kind of self-refutation that he could counter it by proposing a contradiction of another kind:

> The concern of the book, we are told repeatedly in the body of the work, is to explain what is involved in 'the subjective problem' of Christianity—to explain what it is for someone to become a Christian. Yet according to the doctrine (apparently) propounded in the body of the

---

35. Ibid., p. 292.

36. H. A. Nielsen, *Where the Passion Is: A Reading of Kierkegaard's Philosophical Fragments* (Tallahassee: University Presses of Florida, 1983), p. 75 n.

37. D. Z. Phillips, "Critical Notice," review of *Where the Passion Is* by H. A. Nielsen, and *Kierkegaard's Fragments and Postscript* by C. Stephen Evans, Humanities Press, 1983, *Philosophical Investigations* 9, 1 (January 1986): 73. Evans is tempted by the view that the infinite God is something to be known by us but lies on the other side of the epistemological limits that mark our condition.

work, "only two kinds of people can know anything about it": "those who with infinite passionate interest" devote their lives to it and "those who with an opposite passion, but in passion, reject it". Thus Climacus—as someone whose relation to Christianity is purely theoretical (who is 'completely taken up' with *thinking* about it and who has failed to develop any practical relation to it 'either positively or negatively')— is an author who, by his own lights, cannot 'know anything about' the matter which his work is ostensibly devoted to illuminating.[38]

I want to insist that Climacus's *philosophical* (grammatical, dialectical) insights involve no such contradiction. Climacus brings out well what 'acceptance' or 'rejection' of Christianity involves. He insists that they involve passion, which he wants to contrast with what philosophy often turns them into: theoretical acceptance or rejection of the proposition 'God exists' or 'Jesus is the Son of God'. For this reason, it is misleading to describe Climacus's relation to Christianity as theoretical. Climacus is engaged in conceptual elucidation. Such elucidation does not entail that the philosopher who provides it must *himself* or *herself* either passionately accept or passionately reject Christianity. To argue otherwise is to argue that we must passionately accept or reject any belief we clarify.

This raises the whole question of the place of the *Fragments* and the *Postscript* in Kierkegaard's dialectic. To ask what we are to make of Climacus is to ask what place philosophy occupies in that qualitative dialectic. One cannot answer that question without invoking the use Kierkegaard is making of his pseudonymous author.

Nielsen suggests that since Christianity asks for obedience, to analyze that demand philosophically and not obey is a contradiction, because Christianity "admits of two and only two responses from the person who hears of it: either acceptance of its proposal or else offence."[39] Notice that we are now speaking from within a Christian perspective. So is O.K. Bouwsma, it seems to me, when he says: "We get, accordingly, a grammatical elaboration of the language when what is required is obedience and surrender. The elaboration is cheap in that one can indulge in that and enjoy at the same time one's intellectual respectability."[40] Grammatical elucidation and a qualitative dialectic are not forms of religious surrender, but why should they be? The prob-

38. Conant, "Putting Two and Two Together," p. 289.
39. Nielsen, *Where the Passion Is*, p. 89.
40. O. K. Bouwsma, "Notes on Kierkegaard's 'The Monstrous Illusion,'" in *Without Proof or Evidence* (Lincoln: University of Nebraska Press, 1984), p. 77.

lems that occasioned them came *from philosophy*, and if Climacus is a serious philosopher, it will be seen in terms of what he does with these issues *in philosophy*. This was something Conant explained earlier when he emphasized the aesthetic character of Kierkegaard's inquiries, but he seems to have forgotten it now. He says of Climacus's claim to understanding, "It is an illusion because it furnishes its captive with only the appearance of ethical and religious progress unaccompanied by significant inner or outer change."[41] Philosophical insight is often spiritually important, with respect to belief *and* atheism, but it is not *that* kind of spiritual or ethical progress.

Nielsen is tempted by the Christian response to philosophy expressed by Bouwsma. He suggests:

> The character of the religious demand illustrates how Christianity can become an offence to a philosopher. It can generate a kind of offence of its own in a person who prides himself on being able to appraise a thought at arm's length. This he can do when the thought in question is, for example, a scientific hypothesis and the kinds of possible response number more than two. There the response need not be charged with personal passion, and someone's dismissal of the hypothesis or suspension of judgement about it, may be methodical and dispassionate all the way. The Absolute Paradox, on the other hand, disallows that kind of response. Any reaction short of unconditional acceptance betrays a personal affront.[42]

I repeat my reaction to it, because it is relevant to what I am discussing:

> Here again, it seems to me, religious and philosophical considerations are run together. When a philosopher tries to be clear about the character of a scientific hypothesis, he is not doing science, himself testing the hypothesis as a scientist would. The philosopher, it might be said, is keeping the scientific hypothesis at arm's length. A philosopher may also try to be clear about the character of the response Christianity calls for. In doing so, he is neither making nor rejecting the response himself. He keeps the response at arm's length. Further, to avoid certain confusions, he may want to bring out the differences between responding to a proposed scientific hypothesis, and responding to the challenge of Christianity. Here he is keeping both responses at arm's length, and bringing out the conceptual difference between them. As a philosopher, he may see that the religious challenge is such that it demands

---

41. Conant, "Putting Two and Two Together," p. 292.
42. Nielsen, *Where the Passion Is*, pp. 89–90.

more of him as a person, but whether he responds or not does not have a bearing on the philosophical enterprise. Failure to respond does not entail a personal affront in him as a philosopher. Further, if he does respond, it does not follow, for him, as a philosopher, that "all (his) reason stands for gets shoved onto a siding."[43]

We think otherwise about the fate of reason only if, like Nielsen and Conant, we keep moving forward and backward between the demands of philosophical inquiry and the demands of religious belief.

Why does Climacus think that the whole work must be revoked? It is not because his philosophical conclusions are self-defeating. Rather, it is because Kierkegaard has made his pseudonymous author ask a religious as well as a philosophical question.

As we have seen, Climacus's response to the philosophical confusion of thinking that Christianity is some form of metaphysics, a philosophical thesis of some kind—a confusion that is philosophy's *distinctive* contribution to the monstrous illusion—is to show that "Christianity is subjectivity, an inner transformation." But Climacus *also* asks how *he* is to become a Christian. Climacus sees that his philosophical conclusions do not meet, and were not meant to meet, that problem, although clarity will help in appreciating what the problem is. And that is Climacus's role in Kierkegaard's qualitative dialectic—to bring out the limits of philosophy with respect to becoming a Christian. Giving the philosopher Climacus this role shows why Kierkegaard does not have a contemplative conception of philosophy.

Recalling the first chapter, one may say that philosophically Kierkegaard remains within the Socratic task, which, incidentally, he regarded as the highest achievement of philosophy. He endeavors to become clear about the categories that are found in our thinking, such as the aesthetic, the ethical, and the religious. He exposes the confusion of trying to turn religious belief into a philosophical thesis. Yet, as Kierkegaard insists, clarity about such matters is still an infinite distance from religious faith. It is Climacus the philosopher who revokes the claim that philosophy can do more than clarify in this context.[44]

Kierkegaard's *Postscript* shows how philosophy may be an offense to Christianity if it claims to be the basis or even the rival of the salvation

43. Phillips, "Critical Notice," pp. 70–71.
44. I am grateful to Michael Lotti for emphasizing the point.

it offers. When philosophy seeks to appropriate *religious* concerns, "the assistant professors want to swallow an existential thinker in order to obtain blood and life—warmth in paragraphs for a while."[45]

But even within a conception of philosophy that settles for marking conceptual differences, the *Postscript* does not show that Christianity is an offense to philosophy. The claim that it *must* be an offense is made by Michael Weston in his illuminating study of Kierkegaard. He argues that Kierkegaard would "object to the sort of 'distance' which appears required by [philosophy's] form of discourse. That discourse has, in attempting an 'exposition' of the existential dialectic and so a direct communication,[46] presupposed a position *outside* it in 'disinterest'. But such a position is subject to ethical criticism itself; it is inappropriate for an existing individual, and so inappropriate *tout court*."[47] But Weston's worries come from confusing religious and philosophical issues. If a philosopher says that "God's ways are above human understanding" is a grammatical remark, he is not claiming to understand God's ways. Rather, he is claiming to locate and clarify the place that the remark has in religious life and to mark it off from others with which it may be confused.

Yet, none of this shows that philosophy is not more than conceptual clarification or that we must settle for a noncontemplative conception of philosophy. Weston speaks of philosophy seeking a position *outside* existential dialectic in 'disinterest'. He is correct. That wider context is defined in terms of philosophy's fundamental concern not simply with marking off different modes of discourse but with the question of how discourse is possible at all. I will say more about this distinction in the next chapter, but at this stage I want to respond to the view that my distinction is an unreal one. It may be argued that since proper attention to language games involves attending to the ways they are interwoven into human life, attention to language games simply *is* attention to discourse. But difficulties about language itself are not the same as difficulties that involve confusions *between* different uses of language. For

45. Søren Kierkegaard, *Journals and Papers*, ed. and trans. H. V. Hong and E. H. Hong (Bloomington: Indiana University Press), p. 646.

46. Surely Weston should have said "objective" rather than "direct." Philosophy is a form of objective inquiry whose methods, as we have seen, are, of necessity, indirect rather than direct.

47. Michael Weston, *Kierkegaard and Modern Continental Philosophy* (London: Routledge, 1994), p. 176.

example, in dealing with the latter, you take for granted that the person you are teaching differences to can already speak. But in being puzzled about language, what is being taken for granted? Skepticism, at its deepest, as Plato knew, is skepticism about the possibility of discourse. These matters are easily confused, because part of the reason for confusion about the possibility of discourse may well reside in the kind of attention or lack of attention given to specific modes of discourse.

Absorbed as he is in clarifying categories for religious purposes, these wider issues are of little interest to Kierkegaard. Of course, a philosopher may think, because of his conception of what it means *to say* something, that nothing religious can be said. But the contemplative movement of thought, even when it reaches a conclusion I disagree with, is not from a concern about religion to the need for conceptual clarification but from a concern about the possibility of discourse to what can be said of religion.

With respect to Christianity, Kierkegaard thinks we ought to be happy or unhappy lovers. For a religious author, that is as it should be. He protests against the confusion involved in the fact that genuine acceptance or rejection of Christianity in the Denmark of his day had been replaced by a "strife-waged *pro* and *contra*" devoid of passion. Such contentions move in a vacuum. Kierkegaard asks, For whose sake do they do all this?

Wittgenstein, too, addressed the passions, but without meddling with them. It is as though Weston asks for whose sake he does all this. The answer is, for his own sake and for that of anyone else who both wonders at and is puzzled by the possibility of discourse—wonders at and is puzzled by what it means to say something, the various forms that saying something may take, and how these have their sense in the hubbub of voices that are found in our discourse. If Weston says that the understanding this may bring is "inappropriate for an existing individual," what sort of judgment is that? If the judgment is saying that philosophy is not a form of salvation or a substitute for religion, Wittgenstein would agree. Otherwise, Weston's remark would simply be a refusal to let the interests of human beings be the ragged, mixed phenomena they are. Among the oldest of these is the desire for the distinctive kind of understanding that philosophy can provide in the account it tries to give of reality.

Kierkegaard did not want the sense of Christianity confused with the sense of other things, but he did not question the sense that he saw in Christianity and those other things. Wittgenstein, on the other hand, wonders at the possibility of there being sense in things at all. As we shall see in the next chapter, therein lies the authorial asymmetry between them.

3 Wittgenstein's Philosophical Method

At the end of the last chapter, I claimed that there is an authorial asymmetry between Kierkegaard and Wittgenstein. Such an asymmetry is not easy to establish, because a certain view of Wittgenstein's philosophical method in much, if not most, of the secondary literature would lead to the opposite conclusion. An attractive case has been made for a symmetry between Kierkegaard's qualitative dialectic and Wittgenstein's philosophical method by James Conant, with respect to Wittgenstein's earlier and later work. The similarity he sees between the *Tractatus* and Kierkegaard's pseudonymous works is that they were written to be revoked. A systematic point of view is elucidated in such a way that one comes to appreciate that it is confused.[1] Having been encouraged by the attractions of the system to climb its ladder, we come to see, at the end of our exploration, that the ladder must be thrown away. The difference in Wittgenstein's later work, according to Conant, is that our conceptual confusions are no longer thought of as having their source in one comprehensive system, as was the case in the *Tractatus*. Our confusions are seen to come from many different, independent sources and, for that reason, have to be treated piecemeal at every stage in our thinking. But in all these contexts the philosophical aim is the same: to return us from our confusions to clarity about the concepts at work in our lives. We have already seen why the methods by which this is done are necessarily indirect. Philosophical theses are not refuted, as though they were false, but

---

1. It is beyond my present purposes to question the extent to which this reading of the *Tractatus* can be sustained. For a critical assessment, see Lynette Reid, "Wittgenstein's Ladder: The *Tractatus* and Nonsense," *Philosophical Investigations* 21, 2 (1998).

shown to be confused in such a way that the person who propounded them no longer wants to do so.

For Conant, the form this conceptual clarification takes in Kierkegaard and Wittgenstein is essentially the same: "Wittgenstein's later procedure parallels that of Kierkegaard's qualitative dialectic—one of clearly marking off a concept from one of its neighbours, so as to home in on the moment in our philosophising when our words hover between the two concepts and fail to mean either." In Wittgenstein's later work, "the etiology of philosophical confusions is as complicated—and as difficult to survey—as our lives and our language. So the procedure of uncovering our individual confusions must remain a piecemeal one—one of constructing a lot of little mirrors in which the reader can come to recognise himself in each of his moments of being tempted to insist emptily." It is true that "for later Wittgenstein—unlike for Kierkegaard—the business of philosophical elucidation is thus no longer directed only to a certain kind of reader, and it is no longer merely a preliminary to the business of the moral or the religious life, because its business is never finished."[2] But this enlarging of the range of conceptual elucidation does not, for Conant, change the character of the inquiry itself.

The picture we are presented with is this: the *same* indirect method of conceptual elucidation and grammatical clarification is found in Kierkegaard and Wittgenstein, *the only difference being the context in which it occurs*. For Kierkegaard, that context is 'the monstrous illusion', the illusion that led people in the Denmark of his day to think that they were Christians when they were not. For Wittgenstein, that context is life itself. If we accept this latter view, we can also accept O.K. Bouwsma's view that "dispelling conceptual illusions" gives a common logical aspect to the work of Kierkegaard and Wittgenstein: "There is illusion in both cases. The task in both cases is conceived as that of dispelling illusions. The illusion is in both cases one of misunderstanding certain languages.... But those who seek to understand ordinary language and those who seek to understand the Scriptures run into confusion due to mistaken expectations concerning what the language

---

2. James Conant, "Putting Two and Two Together: Kierkegaard, Wittgenstein, and the Point of View for Their Work as Authors," in *Philosophy and the Grammar of Religious Belief*, ed. Timothy Tessin and Mario von der Ruhr (London: Macmillan; New York: St. Martin's Press, 1995), p. 303.

must mean."[3] On this view, the only difference between Kierkegaard and Wittgenstein is one of generality: "Wittgenstein's interest is more general because he is interested in all philosophical confusion, and not simply in confusions that arise in connection with Christianity."[4]

Conant finds the symmetry he sees between Kierkegaard and Wittgenstein confirmed in the influence the former had on the latter. He lists four of its aspects: "(1) his conception of the intimacy of the relation between meaning and use, (2) his idea of a grammatical investigation, (3) his idea that the aim of a philosophical work is to take the reader from a piece of disguised nonsense to a piece of undisguised nonsense, (4) his idea that the correct expression in philosophy is the one which allows one's interlocutor to acknowledge the words offered him as expressing what he wants to say."[5] These similarities seem stronger if we concentrate, as Conant does, on perspicuous grammatical representations in Wittgenstein and equate these with the essence of his philosophical method in his later philosophy.

Such an emphasis has a direct consequence on what one takes the purpose and effects of conceptual elucidation to be. Here, too, Conant sees a symmetry between Kierkegaard and Wittgenstein: "Kierkegaard is after a form of confusion that dramatically shapes his readers' lives." But then Conant asks: "Is that never the case with the confusions which preoccupy Wittgenstein? The *Tractatus*, Wittgenstein says, has an ethical point. The same might be said of the later work as well. What is the ethical point? If there is anything to the parallel with Kierkegaard, then the moral imperative which informs Wittgenstein's writing (both early and late) should be understood at least in part in the light of a demand upon the reader to examine his life with words."[6]

What does Conant mean by the correlation between what is clarified philosophically and the examination of one's life? It cannot mean that there is a correlation between what is clarified and the direction one's own life takes. The reason why is obvious: both Kierkegaard and Wittgenstein recognize a plurality of perspectives, some of which are in

---

3. O. K. Bouwsma, "Notes on Kierkegaard's 'The Monstrous Illusion,'" in *Without Proof or Evidence* (Lincoln: University of Nebraska Press, 1984), p. 85.

4. O. K. Bouwsma, "A New Sensibility," in *Towards a New Sensibility: Essays of O. K. Bouwsma*, ed. J.L. Craft and Ronald E. Hustwit (Lincoln: University of Nebraska Press, 1984), p. 4.

5. Conant, "Putting Two and Two Together," pp. 249–50.

6. Ibid., p. 280.

conflict with one another. It is incoherent to suppose, therefore, that conceptual clarity about these perspectives is, at the same time, a personal appropriation of them.

In this respect, it is interesting to note that Kierkegaard's main interest was in the confusions of those who thought they were Christians when they were not. He does not discuss those who are philosophically confused about their faith while they are believers. Similarly, although Conant recognizes that a person who becomes unconfused about what it means to become a Christian may or may not become one, he does not discuss the passage from philosophical confusion to clarity on this issue in someone who is a Christian throughout. These neglected cases show the important *independent* source of philosophical confusion. The contemplative character of Wittgenstein's inquiries cannot be appreciated if this independence is not recognized. To do so, we need to turn our attention to a wider range of examples.

If we consider the philosophy of science, how would philosophical vigilance, in this context, be directed toward how we live? Some have suggested that philosophical confusion would lead to confusion in *science*, that it might hold up scientific progress. In replying to such a suggestion, Rush Rhees argued that this suggestion seriously underestimates the *independence* of philosophy, the way its problems and how they are discussed come from the character of the subject. Rhees illustrates the point in the following comments on Hume: "I think he was much more interested in the relation between the knowledge of existence and mathematical knowledge as it is found in Locke; and with Locke's reasons for arguing that there cannot be a science of existing things. And he was also interested in refuting the particular kind of skepticism about science which Berkeley had been showing. In other words, once more it is with problems in *philosophy* that he was most concerned. And if he is a great philosopher, it is because of what he did about *them*."[7]

Rhees would certainly say the same of Wittgenstein. Religious issues may be thought of as far removed from the philosophy of science, but it is just as important to distinguish between philosophical confusion about worship and worship itself, as it is to distinguish between philosophical puzzlement about science and doing science. Even with Kier-

---

7. Rush Rhees, "The Fundamental Problems of Philosophy," ed. Timothy Tessin, *Philosophical Investigations* 17, 4 (October 1994): 575–76.

kegaard's 'monstrous illusion', there is a distinction, as we have seen, between becoming unconfused about Christianity and embracing it. That caution is ignored when Conant says that "failure of attention to how we speak cannot be separated from a failure to attend to the various ways in which we act.... [S]ince it is the heart of Wittgenstein's teaching (as much as it is Kierkegaard's) that these words draw their attention from the way in which they figure in our lives, the task of struggling to avoid such confusions cannot be separated from a form of vigilance which is directed towards how we live."[8]

While we may not deny that philosophical vigilance can lead to, or even be, on occasions, a form of vigilance about how we live, it is essential to make important distinctions in this respect concerning the *distinctive* character of philosophical perplexity. If we simply equate 'philosophical confusion' with 'confused living', Plato's and Wittgenstein's discouragement of the pursuit of philosophy becomes unintelligible. Why discourage people from making an effort at unconfused living? Rhees asks: "Why did Plato speak so often of the *dangers* of studying philosophy? Of course he spoke also of philosophy as the 'purification' of a practice through which the soul may be 'turned towards the light', and so on. But he did not think there were many people who can show the sort of interest in philosophy that makes this possible. There were 'intellectuals' enough in Athens who were 'interested in philosophy'. And Plato thought most of them ought to leave it alone: that it would do them more harm than good.... What Plato had in mind was the spirit in which the questioning was done."[9] And, again, in the case of Wittgenstein, Rhees says: "Wittgenstein was just as emphatic in warning individuals not to devote themselves to philosophy.... Wittgenstein might have tried in the same way to persuade someone to give up trying to be a musician. Perhaps he was not always right in his judgements of the persons concerned. But he was on firm ground when he said that there is a kind of indulgence in it, which is worse than none at all. That is not true in the same way of engineering, for instance. In engineering it becomes plain enough if you cannot do it. You cannot go on fooling yourself as in philosophy."[10]

Plato's and Wittgenstein's concerns are with the spirit in which philosophical inquiry is pursued. Wittgenstein spoke of the difficulty

---

8. Conant, "Putting Two and Two Together," p. 280.
9. Rhees, "Fundamental Problems of Philosophy," p. 580.
10. Ibid., pp. 580–81.

of acquiring this spirit, both in a personal context and in the context of the present age. At the personal level, Conant claims to show connections *between* the difficulties of Wittgenstein's investigations and difficulties of self-knowledge in life. But in saying "You cannot write anything about yourself that is more truthful than you yourself are," "Nothing is so difficult as not deceiving oneself," "If anyone is *unwilling* to descend into himself ... he will remain superficial in his writing," and "Working in philosophy is really more like working on oneself,"[11] Wittgenstein is referring to difficulties in *doing philosophy*, difficulties in giving the problems the kind of attention philosophy asks of us. And this is missed if one equates the difficulties with *personal* difficulties. The analogy between working on philosophical problems and working on moral problems comes from the fact that, in both cases, a resistance of will has to be overcome. In philosophy, we resist having to give up certain ways of thinking. But the hold these 'ways of thinking' have is not personal, nor is the source of their temptation. They are ways of thinking to which *anyone* can be susceptible, because their power is in the language that we speak.

Wittgenstein also recognized that the age in which he philosophized was uncongenial to a contemplative conception of philosophy. When he says that it is "possible for the sickness of philosophical problems to get cured only through a changed mode of thought and life," he is not saying, as Conant thinks, that a shoddiness in how we speak is, at the same time, a shoddiness in how we live.[12] Rather, he is saying that an age's conception of what an intellectual problem is can be shoddy and that shoddiness consists precisely in the inability to see a problem in terms other than seeking answers to it, seeking solutions, getting things done. This is a sickness in the very conception of what a philosophical\problem is, one that can be cured only by a change in that conception toward a contemplative conception of philosophy.

It was such a 'sickness of the age' that infected James Frazer's account of primitive rituals. Wittgenstein did not criticize him for his *mistaken* interpretation, but for his *cramped* conception of what inquiry can

---

11. Ludwig Wittgenstein, *Culture and Value*, ed. G.H. von Wright, trans. Peter Winch (Oxford: Blackwell, 1980), pp. 33e and 34e; quoted in *Ludwig Wittgenstein: Personal Recollections*, ed. Rush Rhees (Oxford: Blackwell, 1981), p. 193; and Wittgenstein, *Culture and Value*, p. 16e.

12. Ludwig Wittgenstein, *Remarks on the Foundations of Mathematics* (Oxford: Blackwell, 1956), p. 4.

be. Frazer could see the rituals only instrumentally, as ways of getting things done, just as, in a wider context, he thought of the science of culture as essentially a reformer's science. Similarly, philosophy can be seen instrumentally, as a way of bringing about unconfused living. One might say that Frazer was incapable of wondering at the rituals—incapable of contemplating them philosophically. By contrast, Rhees says, "Perhaps it is that thinking about the notions of reality and understanding leads one constantly to the threshold of questioning the possibility of understanding at all, and to *wonder* at the possibility of understanding."[13]

If, like Conant, we emphasize the symmetry between Kierkegaard's and Wittgenstein's methods and find it in the way both help us to mark categories off from their neighbors, we will not come to the deepest aspects of Wittgenstein's inquiries. For example, in the case of Kierkegaard's 'monstrous illusion', the distinction Conant emphasizes is between the unconfused Kierkegaard and the confused people of Denmark who thought they were Christians when they were not. With Wittgenstein things are different. The 'voices' he entertains in the *Investigations* are not the voices of *others* who are confused. Rather, these are tendencies of thought to which he himself is deeply attracted and with which he struggles. But the point of the struggle is not external to philosophy, as though the philosophical reflections were the *means* to attaining it. Rush Rhees has brought out the dangers in this way of speaking: "'Philosophy is important because of the insights that it gives you.' Or: 'Philosophy is important because of the understanding that it gives you.' Either of these might look like 'because of what it does to you'; but each of them is a way of saying that philosophy is important because of what it *is;* because of the sorts of questions that are discussed in it, and because of the ways in which it discusses them."[14]

Sometimes, as Rhees points out, Wittgenstein's own way of talking about the treatment of philosophical problems does not do justice to his practice of the subject. He shows that when Wittgenstein referred to gaining philosophical insight, he had in mind what effect philosophy was having on a pupil's understanding, "whether his thoughts had got straightened out or were still knotted and tangled: whether he was in the same perplexity and confusion or not. But even so, this places

13. Rhees, "Fundamental Problems of Philosophy," p. 578.
14. Ibid., p. 583.

the emphasis wrongly, and it suggests too strongly the distinction between the pupil who is troubled or ill, and the teacher or physician who
is untroubled and with a clear view: as though the teacher did not learn
anything from his discussion with the one who is perplexed."[15]

Wittgenstein was troubled about how to express what he was trying
to do in philosophy. Part of the difficulty comes from determining
what is meant by success or failure in this context. Sometimes, Rhees
says, Wittgenstein spoke "as though the question were whether what
had been said would 'do the trick' or not—i.e. whether he would re-
lieve the mental cramps of those who were bothered by philosophy
(leaving one to wonder whether tranquilizers would not have worked
as well)." Conant's description of Kierkegaard's method in the pseudonymous works is dangerously close: "For its aim is not to deceive the
reader as to the truth, but rather to deceive him into the truth."[16]

Such talk, even when it is Wittgenstein's, does not do justice to his
philosophical practice. Rhees tells us that with regard to his own philosophical struggles or teaching, "in fact he was never guided—in his rejection or revision or retention of what he had written—by any thought
of the likely effect on the average student, or anything of that sort. His
question was always whether what he had written really said anything—
whether it really hit the nail on the head."[17]

But there is a far more fundamental worry about representing
Wittgenstein's main concern in his later philosophy as a concern with
clearing up confusions between different language games and reliev-
ing mental cramps. If we do so, we miss his concern about the possibility of discourse as such. Wittgenstein's later philosophical method is
described by Conant as "giving perspicuous representations of grammar," and as we have seen, he thinks it "parallels that of Kierkegaard's
method of qualitative dialectic—one of clearly marking off a concept
from one of its neighbours."[18] But, notice, if one is confused about that
use of a concept and if someone then attempts to clear up that confusion, *it will be assumed that one already speaks the language.* That is why the
method of clarification will take the form of an attempt to elucidate
the concept about which one is confused by distinguishing it from others. But what if one's puzzle is about the possibility of discourse as

15. Ibid.
16. Ibid.; Conant, "Putting Two and Two Together," p. 283.
17. Rhees, "Fundamental Problems of Philosophy," p. 583.
18. Conant, "Putting Two and Two Together," p. 303.

such—the question that has worried the great philosophers? There is no question of marking off language as such, or speaking, from anything else. That is why this fundamental question cannot be answered by means of providing perspicuous representations, for what would it mean to speak of the whole language as confused or to give a perspicuous representation of the whole of language to clear up the confusion?

When Wittgenstein, in his later philosophy, said that language is a family of games, his problem was not primarily that of distinguishing one language game from another, marking it off from its neighbors, but rather with the question of the kind of unity language has. As Rush Rhees used to insist, the *Investigations* is, above all, a work in philosophical logic, and other themes it contains—for example, themes in philosophical psychology—subserve that fact. For Rhees, from first to last, Wittgenstein's major concern is with what it means to *say* something.[19]

This is not the emphasis one finds in the secondary literature. The emphasis there is on the analogy between language and games—on the fact that language has many uses that cannot be shown to be related to one general form of the proposition, as Wittgenstein thought in the *Tractatus*. Just as we play many games and do not ask what all games have in common, so we play different language games and should not ask what they all have in common. All this seems to fit in well with Conant's depiction of Wittgenstein's later method as giving perspicuous representations of the grammatical differences between the games.

What this misses is *why* Wittgenstein is saying that the kind of unity language has is the unity of a family of games. *That* claim can only be appreciated against the background of what it is being used to deny—namely, that language has the unity of a logical system, akin to a calculus. On such a view, every proposition is 'incomplete'; it gets its sense from its place in the system. Language depends on logical principles which are internally related to that language. It should be possible to show how any proposition follows from an analysis of the logical symbolism. In rejecting this view, Wittgenstein said that every language game is 'complete', that is, its sense does not depend on its *formal* relation to other language games within a wider system.

19. See Rush Rhees, *Wittgenstein and the Possibility of Discourse*, ed. D. Z. Phillips (Cambridge: Cambridge University Press, 1997).

Rush Rhees has explored some of the implications of Wittgenstein's reactions to his earlier views found in part 1 of the *Investigations*.[20] If we say that each language game is logically independent, it follows that its sense does not depend on anything outside itself. In fact, Wittgenstein held that a primitive language game, one in which a builder on a building site calls out "Slab" to another builder who brings it to him, could be the *whole* language of a tribe. Rhees thinks this supposition is unintelligible. He insists, over and over again, that language makes sense only if living makes sense. One way of voicing his criticisms is to say that, in the example of the builders, *living is absent*. Without the context of a human life, one builder is not *saying* anything to the other. What one has is no more than a regular reaction to a signal.

What features would have to be present if we are to say that the builders are speaking to each other? Rhees points out that the builders would have to understand each other. The person giving the order would also know how to receive one. The order itself would have its sense within the activity of building. But that activity, in turn, has its sense in relation to contexts other than itself. In his later work, Wittgenstein emphasized that to imagine a language is to imagine a form of life or a way of living, which is also what Rhees wants to stress. But Rhees thinks that the significance of that emphasis is not helped and is actually hindered by the analogy between language and games. In Wittgenstein's example of the builders, there is no place for dialogue and conversation. Without them, Rhees does not see how we can speak of language. That is why Rhees insists that the word "Slab" could not have its sense simply on the building site. It must also mean something in other contexts.

Wittgenstein wanted, rightly, to give up the analogy between language and a calculus, but he saw something in the analogy originally that needs to be retained—namely, that a certain generality belongs to language. But it is not the generality of a formal system, not that of a calculus, but the generality involved in a way of living, in which what is said on one occasion has an interlocking intelligibility with what is said on other occasions. Without this, there would be nothing here that we would call language.

In arguing for these conclusions, Rhees emphasizes that the issues involved are still those of philosophical logic—the issue of what it

---

20. I have been summarizing some of Rhees's observations in *Wittgenstein and the Possibility of Discourse* in the contrasts I am drawing.

means to say something. The analogy between language and games, on his view, gets in the way of seeing the importance of these conclusions. One does not say anything in a game, and understanding a language is not like 'knowing the moves' in a game or 'knowing one's way around' in a game. Such expressions seem foreign and misplaced when applied to language; it is odd to speak of 'knowing the moves' within language or of 'knowing one's way around'. It is far more natural, Rhees argues, to emphasize what it is to engage in a conversation than to speak in those ways. As in a conversation, the unity of a language is not formal, and what one emphasizes is not the differences between things but how one thing leads to another. But if one asks how one leads to another, the answer will not be, Because they *must*, but rather, Because they *do*. What will count as 'sayable' will depend on how people actually talk to one another. Or, better, that people talk to one another in the ways in which they do, that they make the connections they do, will show what is and what is not 'sayable'.

Rhees recognizes that there are pitfalls to be avoided in arguing for these conclusions. In speaking of the interlocking intelligibility of language, one may easily fall into thinking that language is some kind of 'system' after all, not a system such as a calculus but perhaps one big, all-inclusive dialogue, in which we all engage and have our place. That is a danger which, Rhees argues, Plato did not avoid but which Rhees himself certainly wanted to avoid. The philosophical conclusion he has reached does not entail that what 'saying', 'speaking', amounts to, in any context, will be something that everyone else must be capable of understanding. On the contrary, he emphasizes the importance of Wittgenstein's insistence, in part 2 of the *Investigations,* that though we may know the vocabulary of a language, we may still be unable to find our feet with the people. Furthermore, one person may be a complete enigma to another. Rhees used to emphasize in discussion, again and again, that we do not learn to speak by speaking about everything to everyone.

For Wittgenstein, as for Rhees, the wonder is that people do speak to one another in the ways they do, and this philosophical emphasis is very different from one that has as its main impetus a desire to pass from confused to unconfused thought. Of course, Rhees has to clear up confusions in his own thought as he works his way to his conclusions, as would anyone else, but the whole is informed not simply by the aim of distinguishing between different uses of language, important though that is, in many contexts, but also by an aim that making these distinctions subserves—to show what is involved in speaking a language at all.

The difficulty in philosophy is to be content with these conclusions and not to assume that the subject has the authority to go beyond them. In the remainder of the book, I will discuss philosophers who, in different ways, succumb to the temptation to do just that. It is easy to think that philosophy can do more than show that language is not prior to dialogue between people, that it can show what that dialogue *should* be. This is the tendency to go beyond a contemplative conception of philosophy, a tendency that is strong in a technological culture which wants to know 'how things should be done'.

In his last work, *On Certainty*, Wittgenstein is concerned with certain fundamental features of our ways of thinking. His concern is a continuation of the logical issues we have already discussed. Given the emphasis on how we talk to one another, the ways in which this shows what can and cannot be said, the tendency to seek foundational criteria for these ways of speaking will reemerge in the question, why do we speak in the way we do? The questioner is not looking for historical or sociological explanations but for a set of foundations on which our ways of thinking are based. The questioner may have passed beyond thinking that language has a formal unity but yet not be content with the conclusions that Rhees reaches—namely, that language has a unity akin to that of a conversation.

In this last work, Wittgenstein discusses propositions that exercised the philosopher G. E. Moore, but Moore's interest in them was very different from Wittgenstein's. The propositions Moore had in mind were "I know that that is a tree," said in his garden of a familiar tree he was looking at; "The earth has existed for a long time"; and "There are human beings other than myself who have lived their lives on the surface of the earth or not far removed from it." Moore wanted to show by reference to these propositions that we know things other than the propositions of logic and mathematics and the incorrigible propositions of some experience such as "I seem to be seeing a red patch." He wanted to say, quite rightly, that we know much else besides.

Yet Wittgenstein's concern was not with justifying the extension of the use of 'know'. Rather, he was interested by the peculiar role played by the empirical propositions that Moore mentions, in what Wittgenstein calls our "system of empirical propositions." These are propositions that, in certain circumstances, it makes no sense to doubt. Unless such matters were beyond doubt, we would not make sense of knowing, believing, doubting, or being mistaken about anything.

The most common mistake readers make about *On Certainty* is to think that Wittgenstein is searching for propositions which cannot be doubted and which will serve as the foundations of all other propositions. But this is clearly not the case. It is not because these propositions enjoy a certain form that they cannot be doubted. Indeed, with some of them, it is easy to imagine circumstances in which they could be doubted, and with all of them we can, in certain circumstances, be said to know them. But these different circumstances are of no interest to Wittgenstein, for they do not raise the philosophical issues he wants to discuss. I may tell someone in a fog that I know there is a tree in my garden, or I may answer the question of a man who is blind in that way. But Wittgenstein says that we would not say "I know that that's a tree" when looking at a familiar tree in one's garden. For if one said that one *knew* this, the question would arise of *how* one knew. There is nothing more to which one could turn. But this is not because the proposition cannot be doubted but because it cannot be doubted when it holds a certain place in our practice. What is ungrounded is not a proposition but a practice.

Yet, as Rush Rhees has pointed out, it is easy to express this conclusion in a confused way.[21] It is easy to think that the propositions Moore has in mind are the *presuppositions* of our ways of thinking. But that is not Wittgenstein's point. He is not saying that we talk about trees and other physical objects in the ways we do because we *presuppose,* for example, that that's a tree. Rather, that we do not raise questions about that being a tree *is what characterizes our thinking.*

Wittgenstein does not suggest that we can treat all the propositions he discusses in the same way. For example, he contrasts our sureness that water will boil when heated with our sureness that so and so is one's closest friend whom one has known for many years. What if I heated the water and it did not boil? I'd be absolutely astonished, but it would not undermine our whole way of thinking. Yet if someone told me that the person I have know for many years as my closest friend was not that person, Wittgenstein says that I would not know where to turn. My whole way of thinking would be overturned. I would be utterly lost.

21. Rush Rhees, *Wittgenstein's "On Certainty,"* hitherto unpublished. I am indebted to Rhees for his discussions of Wittgenstein's work.

Again, think of the very different example of induction. People have asked why the fact that things have happened in a certain way in the past is any guarantee that they should continue to do so in the future. Rhees points out that the first thing to note is that sometimes they do not. But when this happens we look for factors to explain the deviation; we make use of inductive reasoning. But there is no further answer to the question of why we think in this way. Again, Wittgenstein insists, it is not that we *must* think in this way but that we do, that is all.

Wittgenstein says that the various ways in which we do not question certain things hang together to form what he calls our "world picture". That we do not question them is not due to carelessness or overhastiness. That we do not question certain things is constitutive of our way of thinking. It is the element in which our sense of what is reasonable and unreasonable has its life.

What are we to say if people do not think in this way—if they do not share our world picture? Instead of consulting physics, they consult oracles. Wittgenstein asks whether we can say that this other way of thinking is wrong. If we do, Wittgenstein says, we are simply using our standards to judge it. He does not say that we should or should not do this. But he insists that we recognize what we are doing when we make such judgments.

But those who want to go beyond a contemplative conception of philosophy want to characterize the judgment of those who consult oracles in very different terms. They want to say that such consultations have been shown to be *mistaken*. But by what criteria has this been shown? What wider system can include both physics and the oracles? There is none. And if one says that the mistake can be shown in terms of physics, that simply begs the question—it assumes that the oracles are consulted out of ignorance of what we know, as though our scientific conceptions make any conception of fate an irrelevance.

In the same way, Frazer thought that people danced for rain out of ignorance about the causes of rainfall. Wittgenstein points out that people only danced for rain when the rains were due anyway. They celebrated the coming of the rain. Frazer's explanations miss the spirit in the rain.

Wittgenstein's conception of philosophy is contemplative in that its aim is to bring us to an understanding of what it is to have a world picture. In the same way, Rhees is insisting that language makes sense if living makes sense. But Wittgenstein is not *establishing* a world picture, least of all trying to tell us which is the *right* world picture. In this respect, Wittgenstein's conception of philosophy is very different from that of Moore. Insofar as Moore wanted to refute the skeptics, to show them that we *do* know what they said we *do not* know, he can be seen as wanting to establish what is the *right* world picture. This is far from what Wittgenstein is trying to do. It is important in the course of Wittgenstein's investigations to bring out the grammatical differences between consulting physics and consulting oracles, between celebrating the rains and giving causal explanations of them. But we can see how this subserves questions of philosophical logic for Wittgenstein— questions about what it means to say something. These questions cannot be treated in an abstract, formal way. What they amount to can be shown only in terms of how people actually do think about things, the things they do not question, the things that go deep with them. Wittgenstein wonders at the fact that people do think in this way. He wants to show this as a direct result of the questions in philosophical logic he raises. To ask what it means to *say* something, for Wittgenstein, is the question that leads him, in the end, to a contemplation of the world pictures which are constitutive of how people think, act, and live.

Rhees brings out how the philosophical concern with the possibility of sense is linked, in a contemplative conception of the subject, with wonder at the forms sense and saying something take for different people. A technological culture whose interests have to do with answers and resolutions, with bringing things to a resolution, may find it hard to appreciate the character of philosophical contemplation in intellectual life, the readiness to look at ways of thinking and acting without meddling with them. Rhees says:

> Perhaps it is that thinking about the notions of reality and understanding leads one constantly to the threshold of questioning the possibility of understanding at all, and to *wonder* at the possibility of understanding. Wonder is characteristic of philosophy anyway, as it is of the thinking of less corrupted peoples. Wonder at death—*not* trying to escape from death; wonder at (almost: reverence towards) madness; wonder that there should be the problems that there are, and that they should have the solutions that they do.... Wonder at any natural scene that is beautiful. Wonder at the beauty of human actions and character when it appears in them. And in the same way, wonder at what is terrible and what is evil. (We cannot say "wonder at what is mediocre", and there may be something important in this.) Wonder—treating as important— what is terrible just *because* it is terrible; as primitive people may celebrate it in rites: the burning of human figures, perhaps of children in effigy; treating what is terrible as a sacrament. If someone can think of

these practices only as "morbid" or as "perversions"—or if he can think of them only as methods to *ward off* the terrible things they celebrate— this means he cannot imagine how people might wonder at terrible events because of what they are (as opposed to: wondering what neglect should have allowed them to happen, how they might be avoided, etc.).[22]

Rhees is not saying that 'wonder' comes to the same thing in all the examples he is talking about—of course not. Someone who wonders at the magnanimity of an action is not doing the same as wondering at the terrible or treating the terrible as a sacrament. Those who wonder in these ways need not be engaged in philosophical wonderment at the different ways in which people think, the kind of problems they have, and what counts with them as solutions of these problems. But he *is* saying that these other examples of wonder may throw light on the presence of wonder in philosophy and that a failure to see any point in these examples is likely to be linked, in some ways, with failure to see any point in a contemplative conception of philosophy. For example, if one can see primitive rituals only in instrumental terms, it may be less surprising if one can see philosophical inquiry only in instrumental terms as well—as exercises in problem solving or as the therapy that makes one's puzzles go away. This ignores the kind of understanding that philosophy can bring.

Wittgenstein wrote of primitive rituals, such as the slaying of the priest-king at Nemi, that "one would like to say: This is what took place here; laugh if you can."[23] M.O'C. Drury responded to these remarks in a letter to Rhees, stating: "No I don't ever think of laughing, but if he had written 'be shocked if you can,' then I would have replied that in many accounts of religious rites I am indeed shocked. 'Tatum religio potest suadere malorum.' I am shocked when I read about human sacrifice, even too about the ritual slaughter of animals. And the Covenanters going into battle with the cry 'Jesus and no quarter.' But I needn't add to the list for you to know what I would go on saying." Rhees replies: "Please remember what Wittgenstein is writing about here. The question in this particular remark ['Laugh if you can'] is whether anyone could take something like the sacrifice of the King of the Wood

22. Rhees, "Fundamental Problems of Philosophy," p. 578.
23. Ludwig Wittgenstein, "Remarks on Frazer's *Golden Bough*," trans. A. C. Miles, rev. Rush Rhees, *Human World*, 3 May 1971, p. 30.

to be an absurdly naive or fantastic attempt to influence the course of events—as we in later ages have learned to influence them by science. If my friend is always backing horses, and if he tries to guide his bets by, say, the first thing he notices when he gets out of a bus—I might want to say 'the crazy idiot' and either laugh or feel sorry for him. It would be nothing like the sacrifice of the King of the Wood."[24]

Rhees goes on to comment on Drury's use of "shocked." Of the ritual, Wittgenstein states "that something strange and terrible is happening here. And that is the answer to the question 'why is this happening?': Because it is terrible. In other words, what strikes us in the course of events as terrible, impressive, horrible, tragic, etc, ... *that* is what gave birth to them."[25] Rhees asks Drury: "If you were shocked at these practices would you express it in some other way than Wittgenstein's? You say you are shocked about human sacrifice and this is exactly what he is writing about in this passage."[26] Wittgenstein finds the rites frightening and sinister, using the word *finster*, which also means 'the dark of a dark night'. Wittgenstein deems the word appropriate, Rhees argues, because of what enters our contemplation of the rites, something that comes "from the thought of man and his past,[27] from the strange things I see in myself and in others, what I have seen and heard."[28]

Yet the use of 'shocked' may be such as to work against this kind of contemplative understanding of the lives of human beings, which is why Rhees thinks Wittgenstein would have avoided the word: "We may say we are shocked by what happened at My Lai or at Lidice. I would not say I was shocked by the practice of child sacrifice in a really living religion, say in some part of Africa. If I learned that a group of people were practicing child sacrifice in some house in London at the present day, this would be entirely—repeat: *entirely*—different. I would think the African practice was terrible—or I might say something of the sort. But I should have a deep respect for it."[29]

But then Rhees adds, "And I should certainly not say that people from other lands ought to break it up." I do not see that this reaction

24. See Rush Rhees, "Religious Practices," in *On Religion and Philosophy*, ed. D.Z. Phillips (Cambridge: Cambridge University Press, 1997), pp. 100–101.

25. Wittgenstein, "Frazer's *Golden Bough*," p. 30.

26. Rhees, "Religious Practices," p. 101.

27. Rhees thinks this passage ought to read "the thought of men and their past."

28. Rhees, "Religious Practices," p. 102.

29. Ibid., pp. 101–2.

must follow from Rhees's analysis, and perhaps he does not say that it
does. Rhees's concern is that the ritual is not misrepresented, but even
in the absence of such misrepresentation, one may still want to oppose
the rites. It is simply that to do so takes us away from the kind of understanding Wittgenstein is emphasizing: the understanding about
world pictures that comes from contemplating "agreement in people's
lives." Rhees says: "I am assuming that the practice of child sacrifice
means something deep to the people who take part in it; and, generally,
to the victim. There was nothing of the sort, I take it, in the massacre at
My Lai. For this reason we may say that the massacre was vicious sav-
agery, the worse when one thinks of the culture from which the killers
came."[30]

Rhees says he could not discuss the matter further if someone saw
no difference between the two cases. But it is important to see that
Rhees's point has nothing to do with the judgments people may or may
not wish to make. The diversity of those judgments would be part of
the different "agreements in people's lives" worthy of philosophical
contemplation, although there will be a difference between judgments
made with and without understanding. Wittgenstein's interest here is
not personal. He is not engaging in advocacy. He is interested in these
practices as inclinations that go deep in people's lives and for the way
they stand fast for people. If there is advocacy involved at all, it is advocacy concerning the conduct of our inquiries, getting us to see how
problems in philosophical logic concerning sense and nonsense can
lead us to a contemplation of various "agreements in people's lives."

Rhees comments on this conception of philosophy, one that, it
seems to me, shows an asymmetry with the role which philosophy has
in Kierkegaard's qualitative dialectic.

> To do philosophy, a man must be able not only to see questions where
> those not given to philosophy see none, but also to look on these ques-
> tions in a particular way. Not wanting to dismiss the questions, nor get
> rid of them through any sort of answer, or to show that they are a sort of
> needless worry to be put out of mind. (Wittgenstein sometimes spoke
> about this in a way that was misleading and contrary to his own prac-
> tice.) Trying rather to understand these questions—and from this angle
> or in this sense to understand human thinking and human investigation
> and human life; to understand how they arise in, and in one sense be-

30. Ibid., p. 102.

long to, our thinking about questions that we ask and answer. This goes with *contemplation* of the ways in which people think and inquire—e.g. in trying to solve problems of physics, or in connexion with moral problems. And this is difficult. Perhaps especially so in a culture which has become as technological as ours—as much preoccupied with getting things done, with how to do things, with results."[31]

As we have seen, for Kierkegaard, as a religious thinker, marking off a category from its neighbors has the purpose of clarifying the nature of a path that leads to a city whose builder and maker is God, whether the path is taken or rejected. Conceptual clarification and grammatical distinctions subserve this purpose. Wittgenstein, on the other hand, says, "The philosopher is not a citizen of any community of ideas; that's what makes him a philosopher."[32] For Conant, Wittgenstein's later philosophy "is no longer merely a preliminary to the business of the moral or the religious life." It is now a preliminary to clear-sighted living, hence "its business is never finished."[33] But this seriously underestimates the independence of philosophy and the depth of its questions—for example, the questions that exercised Wittgenstein and Rhees in philosophical logic. These are not *preliminary* to anything.

Some philosophers have doubted whether this contemplative conception of philosophy is sustainable where the discussion of religion is concerned. For example, A. E. Taylor argued in *The Faith of a Moralist,* that the religious point of view of a person who does not pray will turn out, on examination, to be aesthetic rather than religious. For Taylor, the aesthete practices various possibilities. His indulgence in them is sentimental, without serious commitment. It may seem that Wittgenstein has to answer this case: on the one hand, Wittgenstein said to Drury, "I cannot help seeing every problem from a religious point of view," but on the other hand, he states, "I cannot kneel to pray, because it's as though my knees were stiff. I am afraid of dissolution (of my own dissolution), should I become soft."[34] Put in Taylor's terms, how can there be a religious point of view that involves a failure to pray? Certainly, there can be no *a priori* denial of the possibility of sentimentality

---

31. Rhees, "Fundamental Problems of Philosophy," pp. 578–79.

32. Ludwig Wittgenstein, *Zettel,* trans. G. E. M. Anscombe (Oxford: Blackwell, 1967), par. 455.

33. Conant, "Putting Two and Two Together," p. 303.

34. M. O'C. Drury, "Some Notes on Conversations with Wittgenstein," in *Ludwig Wittgenstein: Personal Recollections,* ed. Rush Rhees (Oxford: Blackwell, 1984), p. 94, and Wittgenstein, *Culture and Value,* p. 56e.

in the "religious point of view," but there can be no *a priori* assumptions
about the presence of sentimentality either. Each case has to be looked
at on its merit. And anyone who has looked at Wittgenstein's discussions of religion, whether of primitive rituals or of Christian beliefs,
whether or not his conclusions are accepted, cannot claim to find Taylor's aestheticism there.

What, then, are we to make of the apparent tension between Wittgenstein's remarks? Are we to say that there is a necessary tension between philosophy and religious belief such as we discussed at the end
of the previous chapter? Is the 'distance' demanded in the philosophical search for clarity necessarily at odds with the demands of piety? Philosophy asks that the inquirer does not become 'soft', does not yield,
whereas worship is the practice of yielding to God. Is clarity a hindrance to spirituality?

As we have seen in the present and previous chapters, an affirma-
tive answer to that question runs counter to what Kierkegaard and
Wittgenstein hope to achieve. Kierkegaard thought that the Denmark
of his day cried out for clarity with respect to what it means to become
a Christian. He did not, of course, think that such clarity was a sufficient condition for becoming a Christian, but he thought it a necessary
one. Wittgenstein struggles for clarity concerning the passions without
meddling with them. To give another example, Rush Rhees shows how
Simone Weil's notion of charity is obscured by contemporary, prevailing conceptions of that virtue. The prevailing conception has charity
say: "I'm so sorry; what a pity this happened. What can I do to help?"
Simone Weil's conception of charity involves compassion in face of affliction. It recognizes the affliction is unavoidable; that is what calls
forth compassion of this kind. The prevailing conception is blind to
the beauty there can be in tragedy and the compassion it evokes. Rhees
is not suggesting that clarity about charity is sufficient to possess that
virtue. Clarity does not make one yield to charity but neither is it a necessary hindrance to spirituality, because clarity is *a* condition of seeing
the possibility of charity. In certain circumstances, clarity may have a
spiritual significance, not least for worship.[35]

But if there is no necessary tension between clarity and worship,
what kind of tension is to be found in Wittgenstein's remarks? There is

---

35. See "Chastity" in Rush Rhees, *Moral Questions,* ed. D. Z. Phillips (London: Macmillan, 1999).

one line of reasoning that leads to trouble: it is one which assumes that "I cannot help seeing every problem from a religious point of view" is a religious remark in a straightforward sense. If it were, Wittgenstein's philosophical vocation would, at the same time, be a religious one. Yet this religious vocation, namely, his philosophy, asks him not to yield, not to pray. Would not this be a strange conclusion? It is one thing to say that God does not require someone to join a church, but quite another to say that God does not require someone to worship Him.

Is there a way of avoiding this conclusion? I think there is. First, Wittgenstein's remark about prayer and his fear of dissolution must be accepted as the honest confession that it is. But the other remark is *not* straightforward. I suggest it amounts to showing that Wittgenstein's conception of his philosophical vocation is a *quasi-religious* one. Why should this be said? Because Wittgenstein wondered at the fact that the great problems of philosophy existed at all, a wonder that is internally related to the kind of attention he thought these problems demanded of him.

If we call Wittgenstein's conception of his vocation quasi-religious, we do not imply that it goes over into the religious domain. We cannot equate wonder at the great problems of philosophy with religious wonder, because in each case, the meaning of 'wonder' is internally related to the context in which it occurs. The danger, as Peter Winch has pointed out, is in treating wonder "as a given, as something *common* to *the two kinds of* context." That would simply ignore and distort the enormous difference between these contexts. Winch writes: "To be clear about the conceptual position (what it means to speak of a 'miracle') is still a long, long way ('an infinite distance' Kierkegaard might have said) from actually seeing the situation in religious terms. More generally Wittgenstein's philosophical insights into the limits of explanations, etc., even what one may rightly call his 'wonder' at what his investigations lay open to view, is an infinite distance from seeing the world, or human language-games, as the work of God. I do not believe Wittgenstein would have taken such insight as a basis for saying he saw problems 'from a religious point of view.' "[36]

On the other hand, as Winch shows, there are good reasons for calling Wittgenstein's vocation quasi-religious. Often when Wittgenstein

36. Peter Winch, "Discussion of Malcolm's Essay," in Norman Malcolm, *Wittgenstein: A Religious Point of View?* ed., with a response by Peter Winch (Ithaca: Cornell University Press, 1994), pp. 116, 117–18.

discusses religion, he speaks as an outsider, yet his discussion is infused with a spiritual sensibility. That same sensibility is shown in his concern for friends when, for example, he discusses Drury's worries over whether he had made a mistake in becoming a doctor. He thinks part of Drury's worry is due to conceptual confusions, but these are discussed in this language of spiritual concern, a language "poised on the edge of the religious." As Winch says, this shows "the spiritual importance," at least in certain circumstances, "of philosophical clarity concerning the issue raised."[37]

But how can this be said in such a work as *Philosophical Investigations,* in which Wittgenstein does not speak in this way? Winch wants to say that despite this fact, here, too, there is "a spiritual dimension seldom met in the works of 'professional philosophers.'" This is not simply because of the passion with which he pursued the subjects he discussed, but also because of the ways he brings out how "a lack of clarity about them can have grave implications for [people's] relation to life."[38] Wittgenstein said that working on philosophy is like working on oneself.

Yet, none of the considerations I have mentioned should lead us to say that Wittgenstein's philosophical vocation is religious rather than quasi-religious. As Winch notes, Wittgenstein "did *not*—like Socrates?—want to make philosophical clarity quite generally a *sine qua non* of spiritual health," and although "he was passionately committed to philosophy and to a rare degree ... when he spoke of religion as a 'passion' through which one's life must be 'turned around' he was speaking of something different.... He never spoke of philosophy in remotely similar terms." If we concentrate on the quasi-religious character of his philosophical vocation, "it will be clear that a comparison between religious and philosophical questions will not be the key to understanding what Wittgenstein meant by 'seeing problems from a religious point of view.'"[39] I have suggested that the remark gets its point from Wittgenstein's contemplative conception of philosophy.

Winch claims that "Kierkegaard's conception of philosophy was in many ways analogous to Wittgenstein's."[40] But in this and the previous chapter I have argued that the differences between them are more im-

37. Ibid., pp. 126, 129.
38. Ibid., pp. 129, 130.
39. Ibid., pp. 135 n. 47, 128–29, 132.
40. Ibid., p. 129.

portant. I do not find a contemplative conception of philosophy in Kierkegaard. In relation to religion he has something more akin to an underlaborer conception of philosophy. Philosophical clarity serves to dispel 'the monstrous illusion', and that is its role in Kierkegaard's qualitative dialectic—the dialectic of a religious thinker. In Wittgenstein, philosophy is not *for* anything, in that sense; its concerns are distinctively its own. Such a conception of philosophy is not easy to accept. Many philosophers want 'to go beyond it'. Not content with the kind of attention Wittgenstein says philosophy asks of us, some philosophers want attention to lead to substantive results: results concerning what we do know, how we ought to live, what we should believe, and the spirit in which we should talk to one another. In the chapters that follow we shall see how difficult it is not to go 'beyond Wittgenstein' in these directions.

4

Rorty's Lost Conversations

In the first chapter we saw how Socrates, in opposition to the Sophists, emphasized that each of the human activities (the arts) we engage in has its own *logos*. Thus, contrary to the claims of the Sophists, there is something to understand and a knowledge to be attained with respect to them. It might be said that Kierkegaard assigns philosophy a Socratic role in his qualitative dialectic, as it marks out the conceptual differences between aesthetic, ethical, and religious categories. In much of the secondary literature, Wittgenstein is read in the same way. He is a philosopher, it is said, who endeavors to lead us from confusion to clarity by making piecemeal grammatical distinctions between the language games in which we engage.

Rush Rhees argued that this view of Wittgenstein fails to do justice to his central concern in philosophical logic with what it means *to say* something and that his own analogy between language and games does not help in this respect. Socrates does not pay enough attention to the fact that the various arts have their life in a common discourse, a discourse that, Plato emphasized, is essentially dialogic. This emphasis is not in Kierkegaard either, for his major concerns, as a religious author, lie elsewhere. What needs to be stressed in Wittgenstein, Rhees contends, is his insistence that to imagine a language is to imagine a form of life, a way of living, and the role of a world picture in our acting and thinking. Without this wider context, the arts and, more generally, our language games, could not have the sense that they do. Rhees's way of putting the matter is to say that language makes sense if living makes sense and that central to that living are the conversations people have with one another. It is misleading to say that the ways we speak to one another determine what we can and cannot say. Rather, that we *do* say this or that and *do not* say the other thing *is* what characterizes our conversations with one another. These are not timeless, historical distinctions but ones that make up *our* world picture. It makes no sense to seek a further justification of such distinctions between sense and nonsense. One of the deepest pathologies in philosophy from which Wittgenstein seeks to deliver us is the view that our epistemic practices are themselves hypotheses about or attempted descriptions of a Reality that is logically independent of them. This assumption is rampant in philosophy today. It is one that robs discourse of its reality. Yet, this consequence can come about even when one *agrees* with Wittgenstein's attack on it. Ironically, the very attempt to show the centrality of dialogue in language can be read in such a way that the notion of conversation is itself corrupted. The consequences for philosophical authorship are far-reaching, because a contemplative conception of that authorship is never appreciated. On the contrary, it is turned into a parody of itself. In the present chapter I show how this happens in an influential tendency of thought in contemporary philosophy, one that is vividly expressed in the work of Richard Rorty.

Many philosophers, of very different persuasions, think that the time has come for philosophy to give up its epistemological pretensions; Richard Rorty is one of them. Philosophy must cease to see itself as the arbiter of rationality and truth. Its role as such an arbiter is due, in part, to confusions involved in representationalist theories in epistemology. According to these, our epistemic practices are judged by whether they adequately represent something said to be independent of them all and called Reality or Truth. These judgments are said to be the business of philosophy. But, now, if it is said that philosophy is redundant in this respect, the trouble is not that it did its work badly. There was never any work to perform. Philosophy traded under false pretenses.

Once the pretense has been seen through, Rorty argues, philosophy has no choice but to join with other intellectual disciplines in a hermeneutic conversation. Whereas traditional epistemology obscured the character of our discourse, the hermeneutic conversation reclaims for us, it is said, the conversations of humankind.

Some aspects of Rorty's critique of representationalism owe much to Wittgenstein's later philosophy. The conception of the hermeneutic conversation, however, is a direct result of a failure to appreciate how radical Wittgenstein's arguments are.[1] It also illustrates the extent to which Rorty claims that he brings words back from metaphysics to our routine conversations. In this chapter I try to show that he fails to do so. As a result, there is a need to reclaim the conversations of humankind not simply from representationalist theories but also from Rorty's hermeneutic conversation.

The core of the complaint against representationalist theories is that with the claim that epistemic practices must adequately represent Reality or Truth, the notion of 'adequate representation' hangs in metaphysical limbo, cut off from any context that could give it sense. We can ask whether Tom is in pain, but what does it mean to ask whether the language in which we talk of pain itself accurately represents what is Real or what is True? We can ask whether it is true or false that there are chairs in the next room, but what would it mean to ask whether the language in which we speak of physical objects is itself true or false? We can ask whether the curtains are blue, but what would it mean to ask whether the language of colors refers to anything real? Our various uses of language show us what 'contact with reality' comes to in these contexts: what it means to speak of real pain, real chairs, and real colors. What does it mean to ask whether these uses of language adequately represent what is Real or True? It may be said that we need only distinguish between sentences and vocabularies to appreciate the point being made. According to Tom Sorell: "Rorty says that while the world may decide between individual sentences, it cannot decide between vocabularies, and on the interpretation just given of 'decides,' this is true. It is trivially true, however: the world cannot make true vocabularies (or for that matter language-games) because vocabularies and language-games lack truth-values."[2] This comment, however, does not yet get to the source of the temptation to think otherwise, a temptation rooted in one of the most pervasive confusions in philosophy—namely, "that the grammar of our language is itself the expres-

---

1. I came to these conclusions in *Faith after Foundationalism* (London: Routledge 1988), pt. 2. The present chapter is a summary and further elaboration of those conclusions. My views are based on Rorty's observations in *Philosophy and the Mirror of Nature* (Princeton: Princeton University Press, 1980) and "Solidarity or Objectivity?" in *Objectivity, Relativism, and Truth* (Cambridge: Cambridge University Press, 1991). These works raise issues that merit attention irrespective of any later modifications of them by Rorty.

2. Tom Sorell, "The World from Its Own Point of View," in *Reading Rorty*, ed. Alan Malachowski (Oxford: Basil Blackwell, 1990), p. 18.

sion of a set of beliefs or theories about how the world is, which might in principle be justified or refuted by an examination of how the world actually is."[3]

If we grasp the nature of the confusion involved, we should also be free of certain conceptions that trade on it. Here are three of them:

1. An absolute conception of 'the world', beyond and independent of the various grammars at work in our discourse.
2. The relations of 'adequate' or 'inadequate' 'representation' in which grammars are supposed to stand to this absolute conception of 'the world'.
3. The depictions of various grammars as 'descriptions' or 'interpretations'.

Rorty thinks he is free of the first two conceptions, but as we shall see, they continue to exercise their influence on him. He never frees himself from the third conception.

Representationalist theories in epistemology think of Reality as a Something beyond all our epistemic practices. Notoriously, this Something cannot fall under any description. Any offered description itself becomes predicated of a Something of which it may or may not be true. In the analysis of "This physical object is a brown table," 'this' is the x that is a physical object, brown, and a table. We have ways of determining whether an object in a room is a table, whether there are physical objects in a room, and whether the table is brown. But when we ask whether these ways refer to Something called Reality, we are looking for a relation, independent of any context, that has no application and hence no meaning. Bernard Williams seems to be looking for such a relation when he says that we must "select among our beliefs and features of our world picture some that we can reasonably claim to represent the world in a way to the maximum degree independent of our perspective and its peculiarities."[4] He criticizes Rorty for turning away from this task: "He denies that 'deep down beneath all the texts, there is something which is just not one more text but that to which various texts are trying to be "adequate".'"[5]

3. Peter Winch, "Language, Belief, and Relativism," in *Trying to Make Sense* (Oxford: Basil Blackwell, 1987).

4. Bernard Williams, *Ethics and the Limits of Philosophy* (Cambridge: Harvard University Press, 1985), pp. 138–39. Quoted by Rorty in *Objectivity, Relativism, and Truth*, p 8.

5. Bernard Williams, "Auto-da-Fé: Consequences of Pragmatism," in Malachowski, ed., *Reading Rorty*, p. 27.

Rorty would be rightly critical of what Williams is seeking. Our various epistemic practices show us what we mean by adequate or inadequate claims regarding physical objects, sensations, colors, and so forth. But, then, Williams calls the linguistic contexts in which these claims are made *texts* and asks whether *they* adequately represent Reality. This is precisely the confusion to which Winch referred. The search is for a 'representation' independent of all contexts and for a rootless notion of 'reasonableness'. No such notions exist. As Rorty points out, what *has* happened in the history of philosophy is that *one* conception of adequate representation is elevated out of its appropriate context as a paradigm to which other forms of representation are said to fail to approximate. Thus, it has been said that whereas the propositions of logic and mathematics give us certainty, empirical propositions never can. It has been said that whereas primary qualities such as extension, solidity, motion, and so on, belong to 'how the world is', the same cannot be said of secondary qualities, colors, tastes, smells, and so forth. Strictly speaking, we are told, gold is not yellow and lemons are not bitter. Grammatical differences between forms of discourse give us no reason for saying that 'contact with reality' has sense only within some of them. There is no reason to elevate scientific explanation as *the* most fundamental form of explanation. In the first chapter I called this the problem of subliming the measure.

The appreciation of grammatical differences between forms of discourse should lead us to a corresponding appreciation of the variety of forms 'belonging to the world' may take. If we elevate one of these forms of discourse unwittingly, we may think we have discovered a sense of 'belonging to the world' that transcends all forms of discourse. Rorty sees that such a 'discovery' is an illusion. But if he is correct, different epistemic contexts cannot be called 'descriptions' of this 'absolute conception of the world', which is what Rorty does not appreciate. On the contrary, while rejecting 'the absolute conception of the world', Rorty says that the consequence of doing so is that epistemic contexts can have no more status than "further sets of descriptions." But if one half of the metaphysical picture is rejected, the other half of the picture should be rejected at the same time. Rorty does not do so. Instead, he says that it is absurd to think "that the vocabulary used by present science, morality or whatever has some privileged attachment to reality which makes it *more* than a further set of descriptions."[6] But if

6. Rorty, *Philosophy and the Mirror of Nature,* p. 361.

a privileged notion of reality is confused, so is the notion of "further sets of descriptions" that trades on it.

Wittgenstein worked to show that there is *no* privileged sense of 'contact with reality'. The phrase means something different in different contexts. Within these contexts, various descriptions may be offered. When they are true or adequate, contact is made with reality. But the contexts in which these descriptions are offered are not *themselves* descriptions, theories, or interpretations of anything. Williams calls them 'texts' and looks for something to which they may or may not refer: 'how the world is'. Rorty does not think they refer to anything but, as we have seen, calls the texts "further sets of descriptions" as a result. The tendencies in Williams and Rorty are two sides of the same metaphysical coin.

Wittgenstein said that our aim should be to bring words back from their metaphysical to their ordinary use. Rorty would like to say the same but clearly fulfills no such aim. In rejecting representationalist theories in epistemology, he loses hold of ordinary conceptions of contact with reality. Let us consider three examples.

Is it true that in our perception of physical objects, all we are ever acquainted with is a "further set of descriptions"? There used to be a game on television in which members of a panel were asked to guess what object was being spoken of from a minimal set of descriptions. If one could not arrive at the identity of the object from the first set of descriptions, a further set of descriptions would be provided, and so on. After the time limit was up, a curtain would rise and the object would be revealed. In the game, we contrast "further sets of descriptions" with the object itself. But Rorty, when we see the object, a table, for example, insists on calling *seeing* the table a further set of descriptions. But that is precisely what seeing a table is not. In a straightforward way, we can say that having been given further sets of descriptions, we then make contact with the object itself. Rorty's analysis loses hold of this ordinary sense. According to Rorty, our descriptions are always revisable. But when the table is revealed, no further revision is called for. If someone thought otherwise, we would assume that person did not know the meaning of the word "table."

When Rorty turns to scientific inquiries, he speaks of rival theories as different vocabularies between which reality cannot arbitrate. Sorell comments, "Between different theories the world sometimes *can* decide, for example, by making the predictions of one true and the other false."[7] Of course, the notion of factuality in science is a complex one. Account has to be taken of the crucial role of theoretical models. To understand what it means to speak of light traveling in straight lines, we have to take account of a conceptual marriage between optics and geometry. It is within such theoretical contexts that experiments are carried out and predictions are made. These constitute contacts or lack of contacts with reality. One theory may be preferred or modified in the light of another given the range of phenomena for which it can account, the greater yield it provides in the way of predictions, or even its greater explanatory economy and elegance. So the notion of an independent check is central to serious experimentation. To deny this, as Rorty seems to do, is to deny the critical and corrective character of scientific inquiry.

Related issues arise for Rorty's treatment of philosophical inquiry. He denies he has shown that the philosophers of the past were mistaken. He claims simply to offer different perspectives. It is true that opposing philosophical views are not like competing hypotheses in science. They cannot be settled by experimentation. They have to be resolved by discussion. In that discussion, we may come to realize that we have been confused. That is the form 'being mistaken' takes here. If Rorty holds that, like Wittgenstein, he is endeavoring to bring words back from their metaphysical to their ordinary use, must he not think that that metaphysical use harbored deep confusions that obscure our routine conversations from us? If not, what is the point of the philosophical discussion?[8] Rorty's denial almost makes such discussion incoherent.[9]

Rorty makes two additional problematic claims about the consequences that are supposed to follow from the rejection of representationalist theories in epistemology. First, he argues that their rejection has the advantage of "preventing man from deluding himself with the notion that he knows himself, or anyone else, except under optional descriptions."[10] No doubt Rorty wants to remind us that our ways of

7. Sorell, "World from Its Own Point of View," p. 19.

8. This remark would have to be modified if by 'philosophy' one meant traditions radically different from those Rorty has in mind. In those traditions 'philosophy' and 'argument' might be something very different.

9. See Charles Taylor, "Rorty in the Epistemological Tradition," in Malachowski, ed., *Reading Rorty*, p. 258.

10. Rorty, *Philosophy and the Mirror of Nature*, p. 379.

doing things are not underwritten by an alleged necessary relation in which they stand to something called Reality. But the fact that such a necessity is a philosophical fiction is no reason for calling any conclusion we reach 'optional'. What we need to reclaim are the ordinary senses of 'necessary' and 'optional'. In the examples we have considered, once the curtain is drawn, I have no option in seeing a table. I have no option in accepting the results of a properly conducted experiment. I have no option about giving up a philosophical position if I come to see I am confused. Again, we would be confused to think that the way we count is underwritten by a necessity such that we *could not* count in any other way. But it does not follow from this that the mathematical conclusions we reach are in any way optional.

Second, as a result of showing that 'certainty' cannot be a matter of the relation between our epistemic practices and Reality, Rorty concludes, "Our certainty will be a matter of conversations between persons, rather than a matter of inter-action with a non-human reality."[11] I have argued in response: "Perhaps all Rorty means is that to understand what we mean by certainty we must see what it amounts to in the context of human epistemic practices. If so, it is highly misleading to say that when we are certain we do not come into contact with non-human realities. In a perfectly obvious sense, books and armchairs are non-human realities as are trees, mountains and countless other things."[12]

In these examples we have considered perception of physical objects, scientific investigation, and philosophical inquiry. Rorty attacks what he believes are the fallacies of representationalism in epistemology. But, as we have seen, in doing so he robs us of the ordinary ways in which we become clear about how things are. We need to reclaim the ordinary conversations of humankind, not only from metaphysics but from Rorty's critique of it as well.

When we turn to consider the realm of values, 'human nature' and 'human flourishing' fulfill the same function as the 'Reality' and 'Truth' of which our epistemic practices are supposed to be adequate or inadequate representations. An action is said to be a good action if it leads to human flourishing and fulfills human nature. To provide this justification, what we mean by 'human flourishing' and 'human

11. Ibid., p. 157.
12. Phillips, *Faith after Foundationalism,* p. 144.

nature' must be independent of what we mean by good actions. But this 'independence' is an illusion. We cannot justify our reactions to human beings by reference to our sense of the human, because our sense of the human is itself determined by such reactions. Similarly, we cannot justify our values by reference to human flourishing, to human good and harm, because these notions, so far from being independent of our values, are informed by them.

As with the epistemological examples we have already considered, in relation to values, too, Rorty denies that any reference point exists beyond all perspectives by which they can be justified. Charles Taylor describes the situation Rorty thinks we must face as follows:

> Once we believed in Truth; now we only see ourselves as knowing various truths, which don't necessarily share anything interesting in common. Or, if we pay more attention to the detail: philosophy in the modern period emancipates itself from religion; there comes a stage where philosophers no longer hold to some divine source or foundation for Truth. But at first, they fail to see that this undermines all appeals to such a trans-empirical reality. It is slowly and painfully that we arrive at the understanding that Rorty calls pragmatism. And many of us have still not got the point.[13]

What form does this pragmatic understanding take? According to Rorty, it takes the form of a hermeneutic conversation. I have argued that the consequences Rorty thinks follow from his attack on representationalism in epistemology show that he is still in the grip of the very metaphysics from which he thinks he has freed himself. As we shall see, the same can be said of his advocacy of the hermeneutic conversation in the realm of values.

What is the character of the hermeneutic conversation? As adherents to different movements or points of view, freedom from metaphysics is supposed to make us ready to engage in a common cultural conversation that has agreement as its aim. What constitutes agreement is not laid down in advance of the conversation. Neither is the agreement latent in the topics discussed. In fact, by 'agreement' is meant no more than the dominance achieved by some point of view or other in the discussion. Civility is the primary virtue of the conversation. By means of it, we are told, strangers become acquaintances, and

13. Taylor, "Rorty in the Epistemological Tradition," p. 257.

we learn of perspectives we would otherwise have ignored. Those barriers are broken down from behind which we define those outside our circles as "the ignorant," "strangers," "outsiders," "enemies," "aliens," and so on.

The hermeneutic conversation is called abnormal discourse, by which Rorty means that, unlike normal discourse, it has no established methods for settling disputes. As a result, we are told, there can be no place in such a conversation for absolute values or commitments. Even when a point of view becomes dominant, it must not be elevated into an absolute. Rather than let the situation become static in this respect, participants in the conversation must be ready to accommodate novelties as they appear on the cultural horizon. Rorty says that it would be foolish of anyone to hold on to old ideals when the majority are ready for change.

In disposing of metaphysical absolutes, Rorty believes, mistakenly, that no place remains for ordinary absolutes in the realm of values. This is because he is still in the grip of the view he attacks, namely, that the only sense which can be given to 'absolute value' is the metaphysical one. This assumption has far-reaching consequences; it affects Rorty's discussion of what genuine discussion can or cannot do. The all too apparent danger is that the hermeneutic conversation is the conversation of the dilettante, someone who cannot give himself or herself to anything. This makes the hermeneutic conversation a form of skepticism, because it leaves no logical space for the possibility of genuine discussion, genuine agreement, genuine disagreement, or genuine compromise. The best argument is the one that works.

Once we allow people with genuine values to enter the conversation Rorty envisages, the difference will be enormous. If people are committed to a point of view, they may or may not be prepared to talk to those who disagree with them. They will not be prepared to give an open-ended commitment to converse no matter what the topic in the conversation may be and to regard as 'agreement' whatever the outcome may be. Such a reluctance would not be, as Rorty thinks, a failure to be realistic and pragmatic about the times in which they live. Rather, their reservation is a qualifying mark of seriousness in *any* conversation. As we have seen, Rorty's hope is that in the hermeneutic conversation, strangers will become acquaintances, and the barriers of ignorance and prejudice will be broken down. Of course, that may happen in a conversation. But what Rorty does not allow for is the situation in which *not* to talk to strangers is good advice. Some will seem stranger to us at the end of a conversation than they did at its beginning. Some conversations will not advance very far before we realize that we should not be involved in them. Some conversations may not even begin. Philosophy contemplates and allows logical space for all these possibilities.

Unless the possibility of such reactions is allowed for, tolerance degenerates into easy acquiescence. What if the majority are not on the side of the values some people revere? Does it follow that they should abandon those values or are foolish enough to keep them? If they gave them up simply because the majority were not with them, they would, in Flannery O'Connor's terms, be thinking "with the herd." On Rorty's view, if the herd wants to move in a certain direction, others should follow it. But, as O'Connor says, whether the herd should be followed depends on what the herd is doing. If the herd is right, it should be followed, but if it is not, then it should not:[14] The herd may be on its way to the swine trough. The dominance Rorty seems to appeal to may crush what is decent. Why should a practice be abandoned?[15] Think of prisoners in a concentration camp who held on to some measure of dignity by washing daily in filthy water.[16] Given the normal purpose of washing, it was pointless to do so. Of course, I am not saying that Rorty would welcome these conclusions but asking how, within the context of his hermeneutic conversation, sense can be made of the reactions I mention. Indeed, within this context, it remains a mystery as to how people came to have the allegiances that they are supposed to bring to the conversation. The range of concepts provided by the notion of the hermeneutic conversation is too impoverished to provide an account of people's commitments. As we saw in Chapter 3, these concepts could not constitute genuine dialogue or conversation.

Charles Taylor describes some of Rorty's conceptual presuppositions as follows: "What is radical is the promise that we can free ourselves of a whole host of questions which have been central to philosophy hitherto: about the real nature of human beings, about the truly valid ethical standards, about truth in science, and the like. Rorty offers a great leap into non-realism: where there have hitherto been thought to be facts or truths-of-the-matter, there turn out to be only

---

14. See Flannery O'Connor, *The Habit of Being,* ed. Sally Fitzgerald (New York: Vintage Books, 1980), p. 456.

15. For further discussion, see D. Z. Phillips, "What Can We Expect from Ethics?" in *Interventions in Ethics* (London: Macmillan, 1992).

16. For a discussion of such cases, see Timothy Tessin, "Talking about Trees," *Philosophical Investigations* 15, 1 (January 1992).

rival languages, between which we end up plumping, if we do, because in some way one works better for us than the others."[17]

The real need, however, is to cut through the realism/nonrealism debate. We need to appreciate that our philosophical choice is not between realism and a mere plumping for some perspective. I want to show this by comparing Rorty's remarks with comments by Rush Rhees. Like Rorty, Rhees too would combat metaphysical realism in ethics. Unlike Rorty, however, Rhees allows moral and political allegiances to be themselves. He shows us how different they are both from factual, empirical matters and from preferences of taste. Rhees brings out the importance of reflection on moral matters and what being mistaken about them may amount to. None of these important grammatical insights can be accounted for in terms of Rorty's notion of the hermeneutic conversation. Such are the skeptical implications of such a notion that what it suggests is a marginal cultural phenomenon: the interest of a dilettante in a conversation, the transient involvement of someone who looks in briefly with no intention of staying. From such a perspective, no account can be given of genuine commitments, genuine criticism, or the cooperation or lack of cooperation between different movements. There is nothing worthy of philosophical contemplation.

Rejecting realism in ethics, Rorty thinks that the only alternative is nonrealism. For him 'right' and 'good' are terms of general commendation. We call 'good' whatever point of view or perspective we approve of. The terms of commendation remain the same, whereas the descriptions of the states of affairs to which they refer vary. This nonrealism seems to inherit all the old difficulties surrounding emotivism and prescriptivism in ethics, where commendation is thought of as externally related to its object. But unless commendation were related to moral concepts in a wide range with which we are familiar, we could make nothing of it.[18] Because Rorty does not emphasize this point, allegiance to a perspective, on his view, amounts to no more than a "plumping," as Taylor says—a preference of taste. This follows from the false choice with which we are confronted: either moral values have external foundations or they are products of choice. Rejecting the first al-

17. Taylor, "Rorty in the Epistemological Tradition," p. 258.
18. See my paper "On Morality's Having a Point" (with H.O. Mounce) in *Interventions in Ethics*.

ternative, he chooses the second, which is equally unsatisfactory. Rush
Rhees shows why: "(In certain contexts 'I like beauty' may be used as a
genuine expression of moral judgment, but then it is not just an expression of personal taste.) Someone who says 'I see that honesty is
good' may have thought a lot about the distinction of good and evil, or
right and wrong, in various cases. He is not just saying how he *happens*
to feel. ('I feel like taking a walk.' 'I feel like being honest.')"[19]

It may be thought that Rorty's analysis comes into its own *after*
moral reflection is over and disagreement persists. Is not this disagreement akin to a clash of preferences, as far as its *form* is concerned? The
answer to this point is to refuse the challenge to demonstrate the importance of moral matters on *formal* grounds alone, since that is not
where their importance lies.[20] To appreciate that, we must turn, as
Rhees does, to the *substantive* issues involved.

It may be thought that Rorty's analysis fits moral matters better than
empirical states of affairs.[21] In the former context, if we reject Rorty's
view that we never perceive anything except as further sets of descriptions, we can see why, if there are chairs in a room, we expect anyone
with normal eyesight to see them. But when moral perspectives clash,
there are no facts independent of them to settle the disagreements.
Rorty argues that the adherent of one perspective cannot say that an
adherent of another is mistaken. But this is because he assumes that
'mistake' here should be something akin to a mathematical mistake.
Rather, what we need to appreciate is the grammar of 'mistake' in
moral contexts. Rhees recognizes the same difficulties as Rorty wrestles
with but refuses to draw the same conclusions from them:

> If I do think that the man who decided differently was wrong, I could
> not speak of proving he was wrong. That has no sense. This does not
> mean that I am uncertain or that I cannot say definitely that he is
> wrong.
>
> Someone says: "But if I cannot prove it, then you may be wrong, your-
> self; and you may be wrong when you say that *he* is." Well, what does this
> show? Sometimes I see afterwards that I *have* been wrong. But how do I

19. Rush Rhees, "What Are Moral Statements Like?" in *Without Answers* (London:
Routledge, 1969), p. 105. Reprinted in Rush Rhees, *Moral Questions,* ed. D. Z. Phillips
(London: Macmillan, 1999).

20. For an example of my mistaken acceptance of such a challenge on its own terms,
see "In Search of the Moral 'Must,'" in *Interventions in Ethics.* For my self-criticism, see my
introduction, pp. xi–xii.

21. Sorell is tempted to think this; see "World from Its Own Point of View."

see this? Not by any conclusive proof of the universal practical reason. I see it by being convinced that I ought *not* to have done this: i.e. once again by being sure. "We could never find out that we have made mistakes, unless we sometimes made no mistakes." When you tell me that I am wrong, then you are not uttering a logical absurdity; what you are saying makes sense, and I can understand it. In fact, I should not have had the trouble in *coming* to my decision otherwise. So I admit that my decisions "may be wrong," if that is all that is meant. But this does not mean that I must say "And yet I know I may be wrong"—as though I were hesitant or wavering. Often enough I am hesitant; but not on *these* grounds.

Fr. R. emphasized the importance of *responsibility* in connection with moral decisions. Well, exactly.[22]

Rhees also brings out connections between moral reflection and the recognition of one's moral mistakes:

I might say "I don't think honesty is as important as you make it out to be" (which would not mean 'I am not so very fond of it'). I am not telling you something about my state of mind when I say that I feel this way about honesty.

On the other hand, if I had said 'I don't think that smoking is as dangerous as the doctors make it out to be,' this would be a different sort of statement....

It is true that in connection with *both* kinds of statements I am suggesting that the other man is making a mistake. And it is often important to emphasize that we can make mistakes in moral judgments and that one can learn, e.g. "I can see the depth and importance of humility now, although for a long time I could not. I thought it was just masochism."

But it is a confusion to suppose that whenever you speak of making a mistake you mean something like a mistake in physics or in medicine or in a newspaper report.

Certainly, both there and in connection with moral judgments it means that you can be mistaken or can be wrong. (But keep from adding, "i.e. that the facts are otherwise." This only confuses matters.) Then consider how you came to say that you were wrong. Or the kind of reasons you might give for saying that someone else is wrong in his judgments, say, about suicide. This will show you what you mean by "mistakes" in this kind of case.

22. Rush Rhees, "Natural Law," in *Without Answers,* and "Reasons in Ethics," in *Without Answers,* p. 96.

(And of course, if you can be wrong, then you cannot say that each man's opinions are true for him while he holds them.)[23]

Because Rorty's hermeneutic conversation does not allow him to recognize the grammar of 'moral mistake', he finds himself coming to conclusions that fly in the face of moral common sense. Of the implications of his views, he says: "This means that when the secret police come, when the torturers violate the innocent, there is nothing to be said to them of the form 'There is something in you which you are betraying. Though you embody the practices of a totalitarian society which will endure forever, there is something beyond these practices which condemn you.' This thought is hard to live with."[24] But this is not a thought we have to live with. It is the confused result of Rorty's presuppositions. First, the *general* character of these remarks will not bear examination. Specific cases would have to be considered. In a given case, a torturer may be betraying something in himself, which, in certain circumstances, he may be brought to recognize. For example, he may be acting out of fear of what others will do to him if he disobeys their orders, although he knows what he is doing is wrong. Second, even when such internal evidence is missing, when sadism is well established, why should that fact be thought to deter someone from saying that the torturer imperils his soul? The grammar of that remark does not require the assent of the torturer. Third, if self-criticism is not part of the torturer's perspective, how does it follow that there is nothing beyond his practices which condemns him? He is condemned by other practices. Nor are the participants in these practices bereft of reasons for their criticisms, any more than Rorty is in describing what is happening: torture is occurring, the innocent are being violated. What more does the critic need? It is Rorty who is still in the grip of the assumption that real reasons should be independent of all moral considerations. This in no way contradicts the importance of *understanding* what we condemn, emphasized in Chapter 3.

That Rorty does not appreciate the resources we have in moral considerations themselves is not surprising. That force and urgency cannot be captured in his depiction of them as though they were interests or vocations that we may or may not take up or maintain when other

---

23. Rush Rhees, "What Are Moral Statements Like?" in ibid., pp. 106–7.
24. Rorty, *The Consequences of Pragmatism* (Minneapolis: University of Minnesota Press, 1982), p. xliii.

options appear. Contrast this view with Rhees's remarks on moral urgency and necessity:

> I should want to bring out something of the *kind* of importance which moral problems have.... I should try to show how they are unlike problems relating to success or failure in one's vocation (although of course such questions run into one another often). "If I cannot find some answer, I cannot carry on in business at all." "If I cannot find some way out, I shall have to give up teaching." But then what about the moral problem? "If I cannot find some way...." What is the urgency here?
>
> "I shall never be better in music, I can see now that I shall never be a musician." "Well, you'll have to take up something else."
>
> But, "I just never get any better (morally). With every failure, I have found the courage to go on only with the thought that by trying I shall gradually get better. And I have only to look at the record now, to know that I never shall." Well? Tell him to take up something else?
>
> "If you're not a first rate teacher, then you'll just have to learn to live with the fact that you are a second rate or a third rate teacher."
>
> "If you find that you just are never going to be decent, even to the people that you love, then you'll have to ..." Hell.[25]

Rorty promised that as a result of his critique of metaphysical realism and foundationalism, he would restore routine conversations to their proper place in our understanding. I have argued that he fails in this task. The task is a difficult one for philosophers: to let our conversations be themselves. In *Culture and Value* Wittgenstein says, "Anything your reader can do for himself leave to him."[26] This is what Rorty fails to do. Having attacked the hubris of philosophers who think they can be arbiters of rationality in the culture, Rorty himself cannot leave our practices alone. His hermeneutic conversation obscures the real conversations in which they are engaged.

In his essay "Solidarity or Objectivity?" Rorty tries to make explicit the theses to which his form of pragmatism does and does not commit him. First, he denies that he is committed to "the view that every belief is as good as every other."[27] Given his critique of foundationalism, such a view can be shown to be self-refuting. We cannot deny that there is an

25. Rhees, "What Are Moral Statements Like?" pp. 103–4.

26. Ludwig Wittgenstein, *Culture and Value,* ed. G. H. von Wright, trans. Peter Winch (Oxford: Blackwell, 1980), p. 77e.

27. Rorty, "Solidarity or Objectivity?" p. 23.

external standard by which all beliefs can be judged and then proceed to say that all beliefs are equal. Calling them 'equal' would be one possible result of precisely such a form of judgment.

Second, Rorty rejects a thesis often associated with pragmatism: "the view that 'true' is an equivocal term, having as many meanings as there are procedures of justification." Rorty calls this view eccentric. His criticism of it follows from his 'emotivist-prescriptivism' analysis of 'good' and 'true' which we have already encountered and which he repeats here: "The term 'true' ... means the same in all cultures, just as equally flexible terms like 'here,' 'there,' 'good,' 'bad,' 'you,' and 'me,' mean the same in all cultures. But the identity of meaning is, of course, compatible with diversity of reference, and with diversity of procedures for assigning the terms." For this reason, the pragmatist "feels free to use the term 'true' as a general term of commendation in the same way as his realist opponent does—and in particular to use it to commend his own view."[28]

Third, the thesis that Rorty does endorse is not, he argues, a relativistic thesis at all. He describes his ethnocentric thesis as "the view that there is nothing to be said about either truth or rationality apart from descriptions of the familiar procedures of justification which a given society—ours—uses in one or another area of inquiry."[29]

Why does Rorty reject the second thesis? Putting aside a view of Truth as that which all epistemic practices try to represent adequately, the alternative Rorty embraces is to use 'true' as a term of commendation connected with various procedures of justification. But why call them procedures of *justification*? Surely, this shows that we cannot say what issues of truth or falsity amount to without considering the substantive issues involved. No general definition of 'true' as a term of commendation will yield this understanding. Consider the ways we speak of a true account of empirical facts, of true currency, of true love, or of a true God. What would it mean to say that 'true' means the same in all these different contexts? Think of Plato's claim that a lover of truth is not simply one who makes true statements. Again, for many, what has obscured the question of whether it is true that there is a God is precisely its misalignment with issues concerning the truth of statements about empirical states of affairs. Rorty's conception of 'truth' as

28. Ibid.
29. Ibid.

a commendatory term transcends epistemic contexts, in its own way, just as much as the 'Truth' of the realists. Actual examples are neglected.

It is this neglect, in part, that leads to the ethnocentric thesis Rorty is ready to embrace, a thesis that makes it hard to see how we can learn from conversations within our own culture or between cultures. Rorty is content to say with Hilary Putnam and Donald Davidson that practices in other cultures must be judged to be minimally reasonable by our lights. He holds that "the distinction between different cultures does not differ in kind from the distinction between different theories held by members of a single culture."[30] But this cannot be maintained. As we have seen, the fruitfulness of theories depends on the experimental data they generate, data that constitute an independent check. But cultures are not interpretations of anything or theories about anything. They are constitutive of ways of living. We do not have to choose between saying that there are external measures by which all cultures can be judged and saying that all cultures must be judged by the light of our own. Our concepts are capable of being extended so that we may come to appreciate different possibilities. We may find footholds in other cultures by seeing what they have to say about birth, death, and sexual relations. One sure way not to understand other cultures is by imposing our standards on them.[31]

Consider, for example, an attempt to persuade forest tribes to change their way of life in face of certain encroachments on their territory by a timber firm. It took many months for the firm to establish contact with the two tribes called Eagles and Hawks, and even longer to get an audience with chiefs, resplendent in the exotic plumage of their headwear. Patiently their predicament was explained to them: The tribes fought ritual battles against each other; they were sick through inbreeding; Western medical aid would revive them. Areas of the forest could be reserved for them, where they could farm in peace, they and their children, and their children's children. To all this the chiefs agreed, their plumage nodding in assent. So then the question was put, all the advantages having been presented, to which only one reason-

30. Ibid., p. 26.
31. For a fruitful disagreement on these issues, see Alasdair MacIntyre, "Is Understanding Religion Compatible with Believing?" in *Faith and the Philosophers*, ed. J. Hick (London: Macmillan, 1964), and Peter Winch, "Understanding a Primitive Society," in *Ethics and Action* (London: Routledge, 1972).

able answer seemed possible to the timber workers: "Would they agree, then, to farm in these new conditions?" The plumage shook in refusal. "Why not?" Came the reply: "We wouldn't be Hawks and we wouldn't be Eagles." That answer is not open to us, but understanding the tribes involves seeing how it could be an answer for them. Seeing this would not be a matter of judging by our lights but of appreciating theirs. Rorty, on the other hand, says, "We Western liberal intellectuals should accept the fact that we have to start from where we are, and that this means that there are lots of views which we simply cannot take seriously."[32] Of course, to get anywhere we have to start from where we are. But this does not mean that we have to end up at where we are.

Looking back at Rorty's version of pragmatism, one finds it full of unresolved tensions. Given his attitude to other cultures, where Rorty takes up different attitudes to different possibilities, what has happened to the open-ended hermeneutic conversation? But if we waive this point and go back to the conception of such a conversation, is not the attitude of tolerance itself one that Rorty wants to transcend all perspectives? Is not this an example of the kind of external standard he rejects? Rorty denies this. When he advocates toleration and free inquiry, he is not claiming that everyone, deep down, really must have such concerns. He admits that his starting point is historical and that his justifications are circular. Rorty says, "It is circular only in that the terms of praise used to describe liberal societies will be from the vocabulary of the liberal societies themselves." If Rorty were simply elucidating a liberal point of view, there would be no objection to this. He adds, "Such praise has to be in some vocabulary, after all."[33] Precisely, but then the hermeneutic conversation cannot capture the vocabularies of praise, because it reduces them to the interests of the dilettante. It cannot capture the genuine language of liberalism. This can be brought out by a final contrast between Rorty and Rush Rhees in this respect.

Rorty cannot let conflicting vocabularies be themselves along with the criticisms they make of one another. After condemning the search for an external standard by which different moral and political perspectives are judged, Rorty, both implicitly and explicitly, invokes such a test himself. He states that "the pragmatists' justification of toleration, free enquiry and the quest for undistorted communication can

32. Richard Rorty, "Solidarity or Objectivity?" p. 29.
33. Ibid.

only take the form of a comparison between societies which exemplify
these habits and those which do not, leading up to the suggestion that
nobody who has experienced both would prefer the latter."[34] Whereas
Rorty succumbs to an appeal to universal preference, Rhees allows political values to be themselves and stand on their own feet:

> If a man is determined to fight for liberty (for the furtherance of liberty
> in this society)—then fine.
> But if he says he is determined to fight for liberty *for the reason that*...
> —then I lose interest.
> And similarly if he is determined to fight for the achievement of com-
> munism.
> It is not as though "there is something about a liberal society from
> which anyone can see that liberty is important." No doubt there would
> be differences between a liberal society and an authoritarian one; differ-
> ent institutions (free and frequent elections, limitations on police pow-
> ers: "inviolability of the domicile," etc.) and different methods of enforc-
> ing them. And I might describe these. I might emphasize that in the
> authoritarian society 'people are never allowed to' do this and that; and
> I might call this tyranny—although this is no longer pure description.
> The man devoted to order and strong government might answer that he
> does not find tyranny so very objectionable; things like insecurity, uncer-
> tainty, time-wasting disputes, the want of any clear regularity in the life of
> the community, not knowing what we can expect—these are greater evils
> for the mass of the people than any tyranny would be. And so on. It is not
> that he and I understand something different by "liberty." We may agree
> on that. In other words, if I do care about liberty, then I shall want to de-
> fend the freedom of the press, the inviolability of the domicile, etc. We
> might even say that caring about liberty *means,* inter alia, wanting to de-
> fend these institutions and practices. But then we should add that I do
> not have any *reason* for wanting to defend them.[35]

Like Rorty, Rhees does not go searching for reasons beyond the
point at which it makes sense to do so. He does not look for foundations for a love of liberty. Unlike Rorty, having reached this point,
Rhees lets love of liberty speak for itself. He does not replace the metaphysics of realism with the metaphysics of pragmatism. Rather, he contemplates the political possibilities without meddling with them.

At its starkest, the hermeneutic conversation leaves no logical space
for genuine discussion. Within genuine discussion there is room for

---

34. Ibid.
35. Rush Rhees, "Politics and Justification," in *Without Answers*, pp. 84–85.

growth in understanding. But this does not mean that we can dictate, as philosophers, the form or content such growth of understanding will take. What we *can* do is to criticize accounts of values and discussion that do not allow for the *possibility* of development in understanding. I have been arguing that Rorty's hermeneutic conversation is one such account. That is why it cannot reclaim the conversations of human kind: it does not make conversations an object of philosophical contemplation.

In the last chapter, we saw the importance of emphasizing the wider discourse in which different language games, different movements, and different perspectives have their sense. That wider discourse cannot be equated with or replaced by the hermeneutic conversation. In the hubbub of voices of which we are a part, there are proximities and distances in discourse. In the next chapter, we discover what happens when this fact is not accorded its proper place in contemplating human life.

5 Cavell and the Limits of Acknowledgment

In Chapter 3 we saw how the reality of discourse depends on its unity. That unity is not a formal one, akin to the unity of a calculus, but rather, Rush Rhees argued, akin to the kind of unity one finds in a conversation. Language is not a collection of isolated language games. What is said in one context would not have the significance it does were it not for the use of those remarks in other contexts too. The unity of language is found in this interlocking intelligibility. As we saw, we cannot ask, in the abstract, what form this interlocking intelligibility should take. It is not a question of what we *can* say to one another but of what we *do* say. As Rhees points out, it is misleading to say that our ways of thinking and acting determine what we can say. Rather, what we do in fact say is constitutive of our ways of acting and thinking. When we appreciate this we can see why, even though we can say, philosophically, that language must have this sort of unity, philosophy cannot dictate its content. And if we say that it is in relation to such unity that growth of understanding and saying something are possible, it does not make sense to expect philosophy to answer the question, "Understanding or saying what?"

In Chapter 4 we saw the consequence of assuming that if the form of our conversations is not determined by a Reality said to be external to them all, they become no more than Rorty's hermeneutic conversation. But, as Rhees pointed out, there are other dangers to be avoided. It is dangerous to assume that if the unity of language is akin to the unity of a conversation, language itself must be something like one large conversation, or dialogue, in which we all have our part to play. In his work, Stanley Cavell recognizes this, but his different and conflicting reactions to the fact have implications for the notion of philosophical authorship.

If we try to expound Cavell's work, we find ourselves, at the same time, expounding the cultural reception of what he calls 'ordinary language philosophy'. In the discussion of philosophical questions, appeals are made to 'what *we* say'. Early criticisms, such as those of Benson Mates, took the form of questioning the authority of the author making such appeals. Should not such linguistic observations be arrived at by empirical, sociological surveys? But Cavell replies:

> In claiming to know, in general, whether we do or do not use a given expression, I am not claiming to have an infallible memory for what we say, any more than I am claiming to remember the hour when I tell you what time we have dinner on Sundays. A normal person may forget and remember certain words, or what certain words mean, in his native language, but (assuming that he has used it continuously) he does not remember the *language*. There is a world of difference between a person who speaks a language natively and one who knows the language fairly well. If I lived in Munich and knew German fairly well, I might try to intuit or guess what the German expression for a particular phenomenon is. Or I might ask my landlady; and that would probably be the extent of the laborious questioning the problem demanded. Nor does the making of either of the sorts of statement about ordinary language I have distinguished rely on a claim that "[we have] already amassed ... a tremendous amount of empirical information about the use of [our] native language" (Mates ...). That would be true if he were, say, making statements about the history of language, or about its sound system, or about a special form in the morphology of some dialect. But for a native speaker to say what, in ordinary circumstances, is said when, no such special information is needed or claimed. All that is needed is the truth of the proposition that a natural language is what native speakers of that language speak.[1]

The trouble with criticisms such as those of Benson Mates, is that they take us away from the conceptual character of philosophical questions. We do not need more information of the kind Mates refers to. Wittgenstein says: "It is, rather, of the essence of our investigations that we do not seek to learn anything *new* by it. We want to *understand* something that is already in plain view. For *this* is what we seem in some

---

1. Stanley Cavell, "Must We Mean What We Say?" in *Must We Mean What We Say?* (Cambridge: Cambridge University Press, 1976), p. 5.

sense not to understand."[2] For example, Gilbert Ryle claimed that if we say, "The boy's action was voluntary," we are implying that there is something suspect about his action. J.L. Austin countered this claim with the example, "The gift was made, voluntarily." In providing his counterexample, Austin is not surveying or justifying anything. When he gives his counterexample, he is assuming that Ryle will take his point. In speaking for himself, Austin takes himself to be speaking for Ryle at the same time, because his counterexample and the appeal he makes to it take for granted a *common discourse* that he and Ryle share.

Even in this simple example, we find a major theme of Cavell's philosophy: that conceptual elucidation, the telling of the grammar of a concept, *is an appeal to community*. Yet, Cavell wants to say, this appeal is not passive. In making it, the speaker is doing something, showing where he or she stands, and the extent of the response shows the sense, if any, in which he or she stands in a community of discourse. For Cavell, this means that speaking on one's own behalf, saying something, is a form of self-knowledge. Yet, the appeal, at the same time, is an appeal to something beyond oneself. Cavell is concerned with how these two aspects of speech intersect: the alignment of a speaker to his or her world, and the alignment of the speaker to other speakers. In this chapter I am concerned with some problematic aspects of this intersection.

The most powerful and persuasive aspect of Cavell's work has to do with his recognition that questions about the possibility of discourse are at the center of philosophy. Skepticism is the denial of this possibility. Cavell makes important distinctions between the way in which traditional epistemology seeks to combat the threat of skepticism by refuting its claims, and the conclusions of ordinary language philosophy in which the claims of skepticism are seen to be no claims at all.

In the face of skepticism's thesis that we do not know what we claim to know—say, that another is in pain—traditional epistemology replies by saying that we *do* know. The skeptic is refuted by asserting the contradictory of the skeptical thesis. Such refutations are sometimes found among those who take themselves to be practicing ordinary language philosophy. They appeal to criteria which will show that we do, in fact, know what we claim to know. For example, this is how Norman Malcolm, in his early views, speaks of our criteria for saying that someone is in pain: "What makes something into a symptom of y is that experience teaches us that it is always or usually associated with y; that so-and-so is

2. Wittgenstein, *Philosophical Investigations*, I: 89.

the criterion of y is a matter, not of experience, but of 'definition'. The satisfaction of the criterion of y establishes the existence of y beyond question; it repeats the kind of case in which we are taught to say 'y'.... It will not make sense for one to suppose that another person is not in pain if one's criterion of his being in pain is satisfied."[3]

On the other hand, Malcolm admits that these criteria do not provide us with logical implications or infallible concomitance as far as the phenomena are concerned, so the question arises of what kind of certainty they provide. Rogers Albritton replies, "That a man behaves in a certain manner, under certain circumstances, cannot entail that he has a toothache." But it can entail something else: "*Roughly* ... that ... under these circumstances, [one] is *justified in saying* that the man has a toothache.... Or: it can entail that he *almost certainly* has a toothache."[4] In other words, there is the possibility of a gap between the behavior and the actual existence of pain. What accounts for this possibility is that people may be lying, pretending, rehearsing, and so on. Malcolm and Albritton try to avoid this difficulty by saying that the criteria they specify must be satisfied. But, as Cavell points out, we now seem to be going in a circle, because the whole point of invoking such criteria in the first place was to tell us when they are, in fact, satisfied: "If I claim that X is the case on the basis of the presence of the criteria of X and 'it turns out' that X is not the case, then I can always say, 'The criteria were only seemingly present' or 'The criteria were only seemingly satisfied.' That something is a criterion of X is new—to appeal to an old thought—necessary because analytic, and therefore empirically empty. So *what* knowledge does it provide?"[5]

But if we ask what is excluded by the kind of criteria now under discussion, the answer, as we have seen, is lying, pretense, playacting, and so forth. The criterion under discussion is one that is supposed to tell us, in *any* given case, whether a person is in pain or not. And if one makes a mistake in relation to this criterion, we may be told to be more careful, not to be so easily taken in, and so on.

Yet, this reaction will not do for the generality of the skeptic's case. In the reaction, we have reference to lying, pretense, and playacting,

3. Norman Malcolm, "Wittgenstein's *Philosophical Investigations*," in *Wittgenstein*, ed. G. Pitcher (Garden City, N.Y.: Doubleday, 1966), pp. 84–85.

4. Rogers Albritton, "On Wittgenstein's Use of the Term 'Criterion,'" in Pitcher, ed., *Wittgenstein*, p. 246.

5. Stanley Cavell, *The Claim of Reason* (Oxford: Oxford University Press, 1982), pp. 41–42.

all of which imply contrasts between genuine and sham cases of 'being in pain'. But the skeptic denies that there are any genuine cases. His or her denial is a denial of the applicability of the concept generically, not in the particular case. When Wittgenstein presents criteria, they are *not* the kind about which we know what a mistake would mean. What criteria are these? They are criteria that *include* what the other criterion *excludes*. In other words, in Wittgenstein's use, criteria include lying, pretense, playacting, and so forth. In short, the concept of pain includes the different ways in which 'pain' enters our lives, including the way people lie about their pains, exaggerate about them, playact, and so on. To deny *this* use of criteria would not be to deny that *this* person is in pain but to deny these aspects of human life altogether. In the face of that denial, no justification is possible in reply. But no claim is being made either. If someone is cut off from our human life, what is 'said' by that person cannot be understood in terms of it. That is why it is misleading to imagine answering the skeptic with the 'intellectual' reply, "But this is what we call 'pain'." Why should we think that *that* response would have any purchase with someone for whom the presentation of our human life cuts no ice? It has to do with the fact that, in that life, the concept of pain is bound up with our evocative expressions of and responses to pain. The child is initiated into the life of the concept by finding his or her own natural expressions of pain being responded to in certain ways and being encouraged to respond to those expressions in others in the same or similar ways. In other words, the word 'pain' does not get its life through acts of successful 'naming' but through acts of mutual acknowledgment in the lives we share with one another. Appeals to feigning, pretense, playacting, and so forth do not undermine this life, because they trade on it. What if that very life is questioned? How is one to respond? Cavell writes:

> My feeling here is: If *that* isn't—if he isn't having—a toothache, I don't know what a toothache is.
> And then perhaps the still small voice: Is it one? Is he having one? Naturally, I do not say that doubt cannot insinuate itself here. In particular I do not say that if it does I can turn it aside by saying "But that's what is *called* having a toothache." This abjectly begs the question—if there is a question. But what *is* the doubt now? That he is actually suffering. But in the face of *that* doubt, *in the presence of full criteria*, it is desperate to continue: "I'm justified in saying; I'm almost certain." My feeling is: There is nothing any longer to be almost certain about. I've gone the route of certainty. Certainty itself hasn't taken one far enough. And

to say now "But that is what we call having a toothache" would be mere babbling in the grip of my condition. The only thing that could conceivably have been called "his having a toothache"—his actual horror itself—has dropped out, withdrawn beyond my reach.[6]

Part of Cavell's point here is that if, given the presence of the criteria Wittgenstein has in mind, we were asked for further justification, we would have nowhere to go. We are not related to our human condition as *knowers,* because that would invite the further question, "How do you know?" But all that can be shown has been shown. That is why the skeptic is not making a *claim.* For claims can be discussed, whereas, here, the conditions for the possibility of discussion have been rejected. Wittgensteinian 'criteria' do not settle anything—for example, whether someone is in pain. Rather, they show us what is already settled, namely, our life with the concept of pain in which we are in pain, see others in pain, lie, pretend, exaggerate, and so on.

We may think of strange examples that are supposed to undermine our human life, but Cavell shows that they have quite the opposite effect. He gives as an example a perspiring, hand-wringing, screaming person in a dentist's chair: "The dentist stops for a moment and begins to prepare another syringe of Novocain. The patient stops him and says, 'It wasn't hurting. I was just calling my hamsters.' The dentist looks as if he had swallowed Novocain and the patient says, 'Open the door for them.' And when the door is opened two hamsters trot into the room and climb onto the patient's lap. So we have more than his word for it. And when later, in the middle of a walk in the country, we see this man wring his hands, perspire and scream and look around for his hamsters, whom, trotting up, he greets affectionately, then we had probably better acknowledge that this is the way he calls his hamsters."[7] But once acquainted with this phenomenon, we will not respond to him as a person in pain. Our reactions concerning pain mark such a person out as the odd one. Our reactions determine his fate.

These conclusions recall my discussion of *On Certainty* in Chapter 3. There, as we saw, it is not a matter of determining what we can and cannot say about pain but of noting how we do speak about and respond to pain. It would make no sense to ask for a further justification of these ways of life. And *in* these ways of life there will be moments where

6. Ibid., pp. 69–70.
7. Ibid., p. 89.

it will make no sense to question whether someone else is in pain. This is not a presupposition of our life with the concept of pain, but constitutive of that life. It is easy to give an overintellectualized account of our acquiring concepts, to ignore the fact that the 'acquiring' is, at the same time, an invitation into a form of life.

If we were to let matters rest at that point, however, we could miss the tensions that Cavell wants to maintain in our relations with skepticism. There is something to learn from the skeptic's questions; there can be no *a priori* dismissal of them. Sometimes, we can show that the questions seek to go beyond limits in a way that does not make sense. This can be illustrated by the limits of humor: "A soldier being instructed in guard duty is asked: 'Suppose that while you're on duty in the middle of a desert you see a battleship approaching your post. What would you do?' The soldier replies: 'I'd take my torpedo and sink it.' The instructor is, we are to imagine, perplexed: 'Where would you get the torpedo?' And he is answered: 'The same place you got the battleship.' "[8]

As Cavell notes, the example illustrates not simply intimidation in instruction but also the limits of supposition, limits on which the joke trades for its effect. But it is easy to miss these limits of supposition in our response to the skeptic when we are asked why we are so confident that unheard-of things will not or could not happen. For instance, in response to the claim that we have no right to say that we know that words do not disappear and then reappear on the pages of books, Malcolm says: "The reason is obvious for saying that my copy of James's book does not have the characteristic that its print undergoes spontaneous changes. I have read millions of printed words on many thousands of printed pages. I have not encountered a single instance of a printed word vanishing from a page or being replaced by another printed word, suddenly and without external cause. Nor have I heard of any other person who had such an encounter. There is overwhelming evidence that printed words do not behave in that way. It is just as conclusive as the evidence that houses do not turn into flowers—that is to say, absolutely conclusive evidence."[9]

Cavell is well aware that Malcolm would not speak of "absolutely conclusive evidence" in these contexts in his later work, and for the

8. Ibid., p. 151.
9. Norman Malcolm, "The Verification Argument," in *Philosophical Analysis*, ed. Max Black (Englewood Cliffs, N.J.: Prentice-Hall, 1950), p. 280.

very reason Cavell cites, namely, that "such a remark is itself produced by the same hysteria against which it is struggling."[10] As we saw in Chapter 3, the fact that these issues, in certain circumstances, *do not arise* is what is constitutive of our thinking on such matters. We would be bewildered if asked to take these possibilities seriously, not because the evidence against them is so strong but because we would not know what 'considering them seriously' would be. The same conclusions would follow if someone questioned the ways in which we calculate. It is not that these ways are underwritten by a metaphysical necessity; nevertheless, if someone cannot grasp what it is 'to go on in the same way' in mathematics, the consequences are obvious: that person will not be able to count or calculate and will be cut off from those aspects of our lives that 'counting' and 'calculating' enter. In face of challenges to examples such as these, the response "This is how we go on" is sufficient.

But in other contexts, Cavell argues, that response is not sufficient to deflect questions. Cavell, like Rhees, is quite right in questioning the view of language as a set of compartmentalized activities. Our practices and interests bear on one another in innumerable ways and would not be what they are otherwise. But it seems to me that Cavell, unlike Rhees, does not maintain (and may not want to maintain) a contemplative, philosophical relation to this complexity. We need to look at different cases where the question, "Why do you go on in *that* way?" may arise.

As discussed in Chapter 3, the question may be asked of practices in cultures other than our own. In certain cases, the question results from confusion. We equate these practices with our own in illegitimate ways. Rhees distinguishes between the My Lai massacre and rituals concerning the sacrifice of children in primitive rites. The shock at the first is not the same as our sense of the sinister in the second. But we may not even appreciate the character of the ritual, a character appreciated by the sacrificer and the sacrificed. We may be able to see the ritual only as an attempt to thwart off the terrible (for which we now have better means), when it is in fact a celebration of the terrible. When we see our confusion, we are rescued from a condescending misunderstanding.

Cavell's examples, in the main, are from within Western culture, but here, too, wide differences must be noted. For example, he cites examples of prejudice, callousness, or cruelty where these conceptions

10. Cavell, *The Claim of Reason*, p. 233.

are not unknown to those accused of these vices, despite their denials of guilt. In these contexts we have tragic tension, not acknowledgment in its victims. "Some children learn that they are disgusting to those around them; and they learn to make themselves disgusting to affect not merely their outer trappings but their skins and their membranes, in order to elicit that familiar natural reaction to themselves; as if only that now provides their identity or existence. But not everyone is fated to respond as a matter of course in the way the child desperately wishes, and desperately wishes not to be responded to." With examples in which what has been taken for granted is explicitly questioned, we find a wide range of cases: "But if the child, little or big, asks me: Why do we eat animals? or Why are some people poor and others rich? or What is God? or Why do I have to go to school? or Do you love black people as much as white people? or Who owns the land? or Why is there anything at all? or How did God get here? I may find my answers thin, I may feel I am out of reasons without being willing to say 'This is what I do' (what I say, what I sense, what I know), and honour that."[11]

Cavell does not say that answers *must* run thin, but when they do, the practice is not honored. There are cases, which we have already noted, where the questions reveal what one ought to have been ashamed of, and one acknowledges this either by confession or by lame attempts at justification. Even here it is important to note that the same question of the same practice may or may not reveal thin answers in individuals. "Why do we eat animals?" may be such a question. For some, any contemporary answer must be thin; given the absence of necessity, the practice is clearly barbarous. For others, the fault is in the question, which comes from a sentimental urbanization of nature. Even if the generality of this charge and countercharge could be broken down, could not *serious* disagreement remain? Does it make sense to speak of a *philosophical* resolution of it? The negative answer to that question comes from a contemplative understanding of the kind of disagreement it is.

In other cases, the question "Why do you do *that*?" may reveal that *my* practice has become no more than a nominal practice. Such a case was Tolstoy's experience when he went camping with his brother after a gap of many years. When, before going to bed, Tolstoy knelt down to pray, his brother said, "So you still do that?" This simple question revealed to him that his practice of praying was a wall ready to fall by its own weight.

11. Ibid., pp. 123–24, 125.

In the last chapter, Rhees gave us examples of 'reasons running out' where, although everything that can be said has been said, the practice is not honored as a result. I am thinking of the liberal's discussion with someone who does not share liberal values. Rhees's emphasis on 'how reasons come to an end' prevents a misunderstanding of the kind of disagreement we have here. If we say that the liberal and his opponent 'weigh things differently,' this does not entail the existence of a common measure as it would in a dispute between the weight of purchased goods. I am not suggesting that Cavell does not recognize this difference. I am interested, however, in the fact that it is not the kind of case he concentrates on. The cases he does discuss illustrate his conception of philosophy as a redeeming discourse. My claim is that in certain aspects of this conception, Cavell goes beyond what I have called a contemplative conception of philosophy.

Let me begin by placing my misgivings in a general context before considering more and more specific cases in the remainder of the chapter. It could be said that when Wittgenstein stated that his aim in philosophy is to bring words back from their metaphysical to their ordinary use, he meant that discourse is redeemed from what philosophy made of it. For example, 'fetching a chair' and 'sitting on a chair' may be redeemed from idealists and empiricists alike or from those who insist that here we have only 'high probability' and that 'certainty' eludes us. But in this case, Wittgenstein does not suggest that the philosopher, during his or her confusion, is robbed of his or her ordinary dealings with the chair. On the contrary, one of Wittgenstein's philosophical methods is to note the disparity between what the philosopher says and what he or she actually does; the philosopher's words obscure the application the concepts actually have in the philosopher's life.

Wittgenstein's distinction between 'surface grammar' and 'depth grammar' does not find much favor with Cavell. Wittgenstein's point is that the surface grammar of a sentence, such as "I wish I knew what was going on in his head," may suggest an application to us that it does not have. By showing the depth grammar of the sentence, what it does and does not make sense to say with respect to it, we reveal the route by which the philosophical confusion came about. Without that, there is no road back from it. But a person's use of a sentence may be perfectly in order even when he or she is philosophically confused about it. A person with whom I disagree, philosophically, about the use of the word 'soul' may use it as I do in daily discourse. In these cases, and they are legion, a concept about which someone is philosophically confused may be available to him or her in everyday life, thus we cannot speak of the conceptual elucidation in philosophy as the *restoration of community* or a failure of elucidation as a *failure* or *absence of community*. Yet, at the outset of the chapter I noted how for Cavell the telling of the grammar of a concept is *an appeal to community*. It is in exploring tensions in Cavell's work in this context that we see the ways in which he tries to go beyond a contemplative conception of philosophy.

Cavell is deeply appreciative of what Wittgenstein says about 'agreement in judgments' within a form of life. These are not agreements that are made by us, not a contract we agree to enter, but agreements that show themselves in the actual judgments we make, a consensus that declares itself in this way. And when we come across reactions that are in wild discord with these, our form of life determines the fate of the strange one whose reactions those are. So we do not agree to react; our agreement shows itself *in* our reactions, which, in the ways they are taken up in our lives, contribute to fixing the parameters of what Wittgenstein called our form of life. Thus an essential difference exists between a way a fashion house may define colors in advertising its products, and that agreement in color judgments which is not a matter of decision at all but which constitutes our color concepts.

The tensions I find in Cavell emerge when he begins to speak about breakdowns in agreement. He says that a denial of the conceptual criteria Wittgenstein elucidates is *an unwillingness to maintain that form of life* and that, conversely, acceptance of these criteria is *the taking on of the responsibility of maintaining that form of life*. Cavell writes, "In Wittgenstein's view the gap between the mind and the world is closed, or the distortion between them straightened, in the appreciation and acceptance of particular human forms of life, human 'convention.'"

The appreciation Wittgenstein has in mind is a philosophical clarification of our forms of life that the alleged gap between 'mind' and 'the world', which is a philosophical fabrication, has distorted. But when Cavell speaks of 'acceptance' of forms of life, he gives the impression that the gap is something we can choose to create or not. Cavell continues: "This implies that the *sense* of gap originates in an attempt, or wish, to escape (to remain a 'stranger' to, 'alienated' from) these shared forms of life, to give up the responsibility of their maintenance. (Is this always a fault? Is there no way of becoming responsible for that? What does a moral or intellectual hero do?)"[12]

These remarks seem to take us away from the distinctly *philosophical* sources of the desire to create a gap between 'mind' and 'the world' that Cavell, as we have seen, exposes so powerfully. He seems to be referring to something else: to distances and lack of community within a culture that, for the most part, are not due to *philosophical* confusions at all. Furthermore, in referring to these distances and proximities, Cavell seems *to sublime* a motive with respect to them, namely, an acceptance or refusal of the responsibility of maintaining a form of life.

This invocation of a sublimed motive consists of the same fallacy as the assumption that we *make* our agreements. Our agreement in color judgments is internally related to what we mean by our color concepts. But we did not agree in order to maintain these concepts, nor is a person who is color-blind refusing to do so. The point has wider application. If we share the interests and aims of a certain movement, then given noninterference by external factors, that movement will be maintained. But we did not have these interests and concerns *in order* to maintain that movement. If family ties, such as love of one's parents, are strong, the family is maintained, but one does not love one's parents *in order* to maintain the family, any more than one loves one's wife in order to maintain the marriage. Talk of 'maintaining' in these contexts has its natural place when there is talk of things falling apart. Even in this case one must be careful. A refusal by a father to give financial support to his children is not a denial of a form of life, it being a familiar feature of it. The breakup of the form of life would be one where there would be nothing to refuse. Compare Cavell's earlier distinction between rejecting a particular claim to be in pain, and the skeptical rejection of our whole life, with the concept of pain, which includes genuine pains, pretense, lying, playacting, and exaggeration.

Cavell goes in the directions I find problematic because of his conception of the philosopher as a *reappraiser* of his or her culture and his conception of philosophical discourse as redeeming the culture from misunderstandings of itself. But again there are tensions in his thought in this context. Cavell emphasizes the exposure of the kind of *philo-*

12. Ibid., p. 109.

sophical confusion with which Wittgenstein is concerned: "If philosophy is the criticism a culture produces of itself, and proceeds essentially
by criticizing past efforts at this criticism, then Wittgenstein's originality lies in having developed modes of criticism that are not moralistic,
that is, that do not leave the critic imagining himself free of the faults
he sees around him, and which proceed not by trying to argue a given
statement false or wrong, but by showing that the person making an assertion does not really know what he means, has not really said what he
wished."[13]

My criticism may be put by saying that, increasingly, I do not think
Cavell limits himself to his task. Insofar as this is true, he does not escape the moralism that takes the form of calling 'confused' what is, in
fact, a different moral, political, or religious perspective from those
with which Cavell sympathizes. He writes: "But I may take the occasion
to throw myself back upon my culture, and ask why we do what we do,
judge as we judge, how we arrived at these crossroads. What is the natural ground of our conventions, to what are they in service? It is incon-
venient to question a convention; that makes it unserviceable, it no
longer allows me to proceed as a matter of course; the paths of action,
the paths of words are blocked."[14]

In what circumstances are we supposed to imagine this happening?
Of course, different movements criticize one another. An individual, as
a result, may come to the conclusion that he or she cannot go on in the
same way as before. A movement may be eroded over time by criticism
and much else. But these examples of upheaval and alienation seem to
me very different from 'the rejection of the human' involved in philosophical confusions about 'our being in the world'. These confusions
would include confusions concerning moral, political, and religious
conflicts within or between cultures, by which I mean grammatical misunderstandings of what 'conflict' and its possible 'resolution' come to
in such contexts. Philosophical criticism of such confusions would not
be in the service of any particular point of view. That is what gives the
inquiry its contemplative character; its interest is in seeing what 'belief', 'agreement', and 'disagreement' come to here.

But Cavell seems to want more: "Since self-scrutiny, the full examination and defence of one's own position, has always been part of the

13. Ibid., p. 175.
14. Ibid., p. 125.

impulse to philosophy, Wittgenstein's originality lies not in the creation of the impulse, but in finding ways to prevent it from defeating itself so easily, ways to make it methodical."[15] What does "one's own position" refer to here? Is the position one's philosophical position or
one's moral, political, or religious point of view? If we are talking of
philosophy, it may, on occasions, bring about changes in the other
points of view, but not because it subserves them. Clarity need not
bring about such changes. Given Cavell's emphasis on reappraisal, it is
easy to assume that 'refusal to question' is always a sign of weakness.
This may be true in philosophy, but it does not hold as an abstract
truth. For example, Job came to see that certain kinds of question cannot be put to God. Or better: if questions are put, they sometimes
amount to a struggle of faith. In more extreme cases, they may constitute loss of faith. As Camus said, "When man submits God to moral
judgement, he kills him in his own heart."[16]

It may be said that these are grammatical remarks about 'questioning' in certain contexts. Appreciating them is consistent with retention
or loss of religious belief. It need not lead to either. The grammatical
appreciation is *not* consistent with the generalization 'refusal to question must be a sign of weakness'. Freedom from *that* confusion enables
believer and nonbeliever to understand better the *kind* of conflict they
are engaged in or the *kind* of distance between them. The contemplative philosopher is not trying to resolve that conflict or lessen that distance but to understand what they come to in our form of life.

Cavell seems to have something different in mind: "'To imagine a
language means to imagine a form of life'.... In philosophizing, I have
to bring my own language and life into imagination. What I require is a
convening of my culture's criteria, in order to confront them with my
words and life as I pursue them and as I imagine them; and at the same
time to confront my words and my life as I pursue them with the life my
culture's words may imagine for me. This seems to me a task that war-
rants the name of philosophy. It is also the description we might call
education."[17] What does this distinction between 'my life' and 'my culture' amount to? We might say that Kierkegaard tested his words
against his culture's, but those words were also part of the culture. He

15. Ibid., pp. 175–76.

16. Albert Camus, *The Rebel*, trans. Anthony Bower (Harmondsworth: Peregrine
Books, 1962), p. 57.

17. Cavell, *The Claim of Reason*, p. 125.

called on resources, however small a remnant they might be, to remind people of a Christianity forsaken by the culture at large.

Cavell, with his emphasis on reappraisal, has in mind examples in which conventions slacken as a result of questions that extend concepts in new directions. He says that the most serious writers have tried to chronicle different ways in which a gap between mind and world can occur. This would apply, presumably, to the revolutionary or the genius in science or music. Yet, the way such people extend previous ways of doing things is itself a well-known cultural phenomenon. Such people may feel that there is a gap between them and their world, but *that* is not the gap between 'mind' and 'the world' by which philosophers have obscured 'our being in the world'. The difficulty is that Cavell runs together *very different* situations that could be described as a slackening of the conviction that I belong to my world:

> What happens if this conviction slackens? As in Kafka and Beckett; as thematically in Thoreau and Marx and Kierkegaard and Nietzsche; as sometimes in Rousseau; as in Descartes when he recognises that voicing his doubts may put him with lunatics or fools. In such straits, perhaps you write for everybody and nobody; for an all but unimaginable future; in pseudonyms for the anonymous; in an album which is haunted by pictures and peopled with voices. But what happens if you are not a writer; if you lack *that* way of embodying, accounting for, a slackened conviction in a community, and of staking your own (in imagination, in a world of works)? What happens if all you want to do is talk and words fail you? [18]

In this paragraph we can distinguish the following: depictions of a breakdown in the use of certain concepts (Kafka, Beckett); social critiques of various kinds and the advocacy of different modes of the spirit (Thoreau, Marx, Nietzsche); a critique of confusions concerning Christianity (Kierkegaard); methodological, philosophical doubt (Descartes); the futuristic visionary; the struggle with philosophical pictures and voices that distort our sense of the human (Wittgenstein); and the plight of the inarticulate who cannot be heard. These cases call for different responses, with a further variety within each category of response. Some categories are personal, as others are not; some are social and political, as others are not; some are religious, and others are not; some are revolutionary, whereas others are not; and so on. We

18. Ibid., pp. 109–10.

need to distinguish between personal, moral, political, and religious problems, despite overlaps between them. Disagreements in these contexts may indicate a lack of community in Cavell's sense, but in another sense, these distances and disagreements are themselves features of our culture.

I have already acknowledged that philosophical distinctions may be made in the service of any of these interests. I have also emphasized that this is quite different from a contemplative conception of philosophy, in which the interests themselves come from the fundamental questions of philosophy. The danger in Cavell's conception of the philosopher as a reappraiser is that it runs these two contexts into each other. It is easy to think that the conceptual distinctions that are made in the service of certain interests are the only ones which *could* be made, or even that the interests in question are somehow sanctioned by philosophy in a way others are not. This danger can be illustrated if we look at Cavell's treatment of moral, aesthetic, political, literary, psychoanalytic, and religious questions.

Modernity is characterized by its fragmentary character; a common discourse cannot be taken for granted. In such times, the recovery of discourse and hence of community assumes an even greater importance than it has in more settled times. Yet, how is this possible when disagreements are so evident in human life? Is it not futile to pretend that there can be any 'coming together' in this context? The differences seem to leave no room for reasoned discourse between them. But in aesthetic, moral, and political contexts, Cavell wants to combat the charge of irrationality, a charge that comes about, he argues, through an overconcentration on those areas in which disagreement occurs.

Cavell argues that where aesthetic judgment is called for, agreement is aimed for, otherwise there would be no point in making the judgment. That view is too sweeping. We can distinguish between lack of style and difference in style between cultures, as well as within Western art. Wittgenstein asks whether we can adopt a style of painting at will, say, the Egyptian. Again, in Western art, there may be times when we realize that we can no longer look at certain paintings in the way their original audiences did. Yet, we may feel no inclination to judge those audiences. In other cases, of course, we may endeavor to show that one artistic treatment is deeper than another and be concerned if that judgment is not shared. In more extreme cases, we may say that anyone who can condone *that* is bereft of taste, no matter how much institutional backing it has. In the visual arts, Robert Hughes in art criticism and B. R. Tilghman in philosophical aesthetics have argued that a rupture occurs in avant-garde work in the twentieth century that is produced in the name of antiart.[19] For the first time in the history of art, a movement is not reassessed by the children of its original critics, as happened in the case of Impressionism and other movements.

Where morality is concerned, Cavell's argument is different. He says that although agreement is desirable, its absence does not render moral judgments irrational. Moral differences are compatible with rationality. How is this possible? Of course not *any* consideration can be called moral; that *would* be irrational. Cavell argues that although we may refute the emphasis others give to certain moral considerations, we cannot deny their relevance. The differences will be respected. This is made possible by an act of moral imagination. This mutual respect, Cavell argues, testifies to the presence of community even when common agreement is absent.

Moral discussion, for Cavell, is a matter of self-discovery. It concerns not simply what our interests are but also what they ought to be. Considerations may be put to us that we cannot appropriate. Thus we find out where we stand. Discussion with others will reveal the extent of the community that exists between ourselves and them.

In these arguments, Cavell's desire to maintain internal connections between the philosophical recovery of concepts and recovering community leads him to ignore the raggedness of the moral phenomena he is discussing. He is quite right to point out that through moral discussion, we may come to appreciate better the consequences of our actions. We may also come to appreciate possibilities we had not thought of before.

All this may be the result of moral imagination. But Cavell admits that moral differences will still remain. What he does not emphasize is that when moral considerations are rejected, this may not be due to lack of imagination. The considerations may be ruled out morally. It is a lack of philosophical imagination not to give *that* fact the attention it deserves.

Further, moral differences may not be simply a matter of the priority given to moral alternatives but also a question of what is to count as

19. See Robert Hughes, *The Shock of the New* (London: Thames and Hudson, 1991), and B. R. Tilghman, *But Is It Art?* (Oxford: Blackwell, 1984).

an alternative in the first place. And even when other people's moral points of view are recognized, why should they evoke respect? The fact is that some will evoke respect, whereas others will not, but which will do what will vary between individuals. Something may be regarded as all the more despicable for being a morality.

Cavell's emphasis on community and mutual respect prevents him from appreciating the raggedness of the situation. But philosophical contemplation of this raggedness is essential to an understanding of how things are in moral matters and of how they enter our lives. As Wittgenstein said in his discussion of ethics with Rhees, the difficulty is to accept that the reasons people give us in moral discussions really *are* their reasons and not something else we suppose they must be, such as the reasons that would satisfy us.[20] That is a lesson Cavell, too, finds hard to accept.

When Cavell turns to politics, he claims that the patterns of argument are closer to those of aesthetics than to those of morals. The aim is agreement. In an imaginative account of social contract theory, Cavell rightly jettisons the notion of prior consent on which the contract is supposed to be based, in favor of a notion of political consensus that shows itself in what a community is or is not prepared to recognize as politically acceptable. Here, when I speak for myself, I am speaking for the community at the same time. Cavell notes that agreement may not be forthcoming and, in extreme cases, the speaker may have to dissent, perhaps in acts of civil disobedience. In this eventuality, the person is saying of what goes on around him, "This is not mine." But, again, Cavell wants to emphasize how, through discussion, there is a constant interplay between what I see around me and what I can accept—a dialectical exchange between a person as a citizen and a person as a sovereign, as part of the society for which he or she is responsible. Little wonder that Rousseau turns out to be the political philosopher Cavell admires most. As in the moral case, Cavell invokes a respect for differences as that which enables one to speak of the presence of community.

But, as in the moral case, things are more ragged than Cavell acknowledges. Relations between political movements may or may not involve respect. Cavell agrees that politics is only one pattern of discourse

20. See Rush Rhees, "Some Developments in Wittgenstein's View of Ethics," *Philosophical Review* 74, 1 (1965).

and that it intersects with many others. That makes it all the more necessary to recognize that different movements stand in cooperative and noncooperative relations to one another. Toleration need not entail respect. And, as we saw in discussing Rorty in the last chapter, even if movements have to tolerate one another through necessity, it does not follow that what they value most is either that tolerance or those matters on which they agree to compromise.

Again, it is important to distinguish between the philosophical contemplation of the fact that this is how things are in politics and the substantive relations political movements may have to one another. Cavell is in danger of running these together in his liberal analysis of political consensus. By contrast, one can repeat Rush Rhees's comment: "Nor can it be said that 'society could not go on' if people insisted on pressing sectional interests. That is how society does go on."[21]

It becomes evident that Cavell is reflecting, for the most part, on a certain *kind* of society, one that he takes ours to be: "Society ... is what we have done with the success of Locke and the others in removing the divine right of kings and placing political authority in our consent to be governed together.... The essential message of the idea of a social contract is that political institutions require justification, that they are absolutely without sanctity, that power over us is held on trust from us, that institutions have no authority other than the authority we lend them, that we are their architects, that they are therefore artifacts, that there are laws or ends, of nature or justice, in terms of which they are to be tested. They are experiments."[22]

These remarks are illustrative of how far removed Cavell is here from a contemplative conception of philosophy. Apart from the fact that the society he is talking of is more varied than his analysis allows (and not because we are all struggling to realize the general will), his analysis does not raise the issue recognized so profoundly elsewhere by Cavell, that skepticism challenges the very possibility of political obligation. But that possibility is not tied to any other particular form of political organization, hence the brilliance of Hume's essay "Of the Original Contract" in emphasizing this. Hume saw clearly, as Cavell does not, that the divine right of kings is one form political consent may take, not a species of confusion from which Locke rescued us.

21. Rush Rhees, *Without Answers*, ed. D. Z. Phillips (London: Routledge, 1969), p. 57.

22. Stanley Cavell, *The Senses of Walden: An Expanded Edition* (San Francisco: North Point Press, 1981), p. 82.

When Cavell says that institutions have no authority over us other than
that which we lend them, from what resources does the authority we
lend emanate? When Locke criticized other parties, he did so in *political*
terms. If institutions are political in themselves, they cannot be tested in
terms of neutral conceptions of nature or justice, because those notions
will themselves be informed by political ideas. Political institutions are
not experiments but are constitutive of certain ideas in terms of which
discussion is carried on. They are overthrown, sometimes, because, at a
certain period, they are accused of not being faithful to these ideas or
because they are eroded or overthrown by political ideas of other kinds.
The contemplation of political agreement and disagreement needs to
acknowledge that fact and not try to get behind the phenomena to
some basic set of interests or ideas that they are supposed to serve.

Stephen Mulhall claims that what Cavell is analyzing is a brand of
contract liberalism, with its appeal to mutual respect in our disagreements and agreements.[23] But does Cavell perceive this? I suggest not.
Instead, he takes himself to be showing that his analysis of mutual acknowledgment or the lack of it in aesthetic, moral, and political contexts is a condition for speech and agency *tout court*.

Furthermore, Mulhall's 'placement' of Cavell's philosophical method
does not rescue Cavell from the difficulties we have encountered. Mulhall claims that Cavell's link with ordinary language philosophy can be
shown by the fact that if analysis is not analysis of timeless moral, political, and religious principles, Cavell can claim to be analyzing and understanding what our present condition actually is. Admittedly, he
neglects non-Western political traditions and nonliberal Western traditions such as socialism and Christianity, but these criticisms would not
call his philosophical method into doubt.

What might do so, however, is the claim that Cavell's method de-
parts from the view of philosophy as detached inquiry, the contemplative conception of philosophy exemplified in the Wittgensteinian "refusal to advance particular theses (and) its self-imposed restriction to
descriptions of that which we cannot fail to know, and its reiterated refusal of the desire to construct philosophical systems." Mulhall does
not think it does, although he quarrels with the view that this method
is a twentieth-century phenomenon. He argues that "the fact that a
method demands a certain species of detachment or neutrality from its

23. Stephen Mulhall, *Stanley Cavell: Philosophy's Recounting of the Ordinary* (Oxford:
Clarendon Press, 1994).

practitioners does not entail that the method itself is detached from or neutral between the wider cultural forces and movements within which it operates." That wider movement, for Mulhall, which has "a classically liberal physiognomy," originates at the time of the Reformation.[24] This analysis may well apply to Cavell's method.

It is evident from Chapter 7, however, that what I have called a contemplative conception of philosophy is as old as the pre-Socratics. This is the tradition in which Wittgenstein stands. He insisted that he was tackling the same questions that bothered Plato, who was concerned with the conditions of the possibility of discourse. The liberalism exemplified in Cavell's analysis would be *one* form political discourse may take, and it is *as such* that it enters into Wittgensteinian reflection. In Cavell, by contrast, we have seen how the form of his analysis is sometimes dictated by liberal interests. This is all the more difficult to detect because of 'the openness' that belongs to liberalism itself. In the last chapter, I argued that even that liberalism is distorted in Rorty's analysis. This is not true in Cavell or in Martha Nussbaum's work, which I shall consider later, but in a way, this fact makes it all the more difficult, but all the more essential, to acknowledge that the detachment or openness of contemplative, philosophical reflection is wider than the detachment and openness of liberalism. Thus, although we do not find a philosophical system in Cavell, we do find substantive moral, political, and religious theses. These, above all, constitute his departure from Wittgenstein's methods, and it is also these which became more and more prominent in his later work.

In the fourth part of *The Claim of Reason*, Cavell no longer asserts that he is expounding Wittgenstein. It is here, according to Richard Fleming, that Cavell, by going beyond Wittgenstein, offers a new direction for contemporary philosophy.[25] These directions are appreciated by Mulhall, but he wonders whether Cavell is now elucidating specific aspirations in them, rather than making purely grammatical observations. Mulhall is certainly correct to wonder thus, but I want to emphasize that Cavell is also forsaking a contemplative conception of philosophy in favor of giving the aspirations he advocates a philosophical justification that cannot be sustained.

Cavell wants to argue that the fact that skepticism does not put forward an intelligible claim does not mean that it does not pose a threat.

24. Ibid., p. 74.
25. See Richard Fleming, *The State of Philosophy* (Lewisburg: Bucknell University Press, 1993).

On the contrary, skepticism reveals a powerful truth about our condition: it shows that our forms of life do not have any metaphysical foundations. Essentially, they depend on us and on our agreements with one another that exhibit mutual acknowledgment. Our acknowledgment of the pain of others serves as an example. This acknowledgment is evidenced in the pity shown for others. In my pity, I show where I stand and, at the same time, allow myself to be read by the situation that confronts me. Cavell has a novel reading of the private language argument, seeing it as a fantasy in which an individual wants to hide himself or herself from the readings of other people as much as the individual refuses to read those others.

Difficulties arise for these comments which are similar to those discussed earlier in the chapter in relation to Cavell's notion of maintaining a form of life. I accused him of subliming the notion of maintenance, and the same thing happens in his notion of acknowledgment. Acknowledgment and lack of acknowledgment of the sufferings of others are features of human life. It is quite a different matter to speak of acknowledgment or lack of acknowledgment of human life as such, which makes them look like activities outside our forms of life. In this context, Cavell seems to be forgetting his own important distinction between criteria which show whether *this* person is in pain and Wittgensteinian criteria which display our life with the concept of pain, which includes our acknowledgment and lack of acknowledgment. That these responses and lack of responses are what they are is what constitutes the form of life in question.

Cavell makes use of his notion of acknowledgment in his readings of literature and film. Texts such as *Othello* and *King Lear* are read in this way. Lear's inability to respond to the love of his youngest daughter denies an aspect of her by denying that love's reality. The failure of acknowledgment is itself a manifestation of the impulse to skepticism. Cavell's ambitions for such readings are far-reaching. He argues that the fictional examples should not be called incomplete. According to Cavell, what the theater shows is the possibility of recovery from criticism, and his hope is "that such a localized recovery can be extended into the world outside theater."[26]

There is no objection to these specific readings as long as one does not generalize from them. Take the very different example of Lady

26. Mulhall, *Stanley Cavell*, p. 201.

Macbeth. Murder could be seen as the limiting case of a refusal to recognize humanity in another. Lady Macbeth's madness can be read as the result of this lack of acknowledgment—the realization of what murder is. Her ambition can also be read as a failure to acknowledge anyone who stands in its way. This is pretty much the standard reading.

My late colleague D.L. Sims, in an unpublished paper, offered a much deeper reading. Lady Macbeth saw, from the start, what her husband wanted: he wanted blood. She loved Macbeth with such a terrible love that she allowed the monster in him to emerge into the light of day, although the price of its emergence was her own madness. Her fate is not the result of failure of acknowledgment but of an all too correct acknowledgment—that of the terrible. Macbeth, it might be said, tries to turn it into something splendid, but not his wife.

Mulhall counters the charge of selectivity of texts by saying that "anyone who understands the acknowledgement structure underlying Cavell's model of reading would expect him to search for and to use texts which participate in his own attitude and approach to reading for according to the terms of that approach, only texts written in the spirit in which he reads would be capable of calling forth heightened or exemplary experiences of reading—only texts motivated by the thoughts and feelings that are crystallized in Cavell's own conception and practice of reading could provide words capable of testing and drawing out the full potential of that practice."[27] Because Cavell's examples from literature are selective, illustrative of the kinds of acknowledgment and lack of acknowledgment he discusses, of course they draw out the full potential of those notions. But in what sense does it *test* them? Certainly not by establishing that these readings are superior to readings of *other* texts that would reflect other circumstances in human life. A contemplative conception of philosophy takes account of these different possibilities.

A further development in Cavell's later thought threatens to be an obstacle to such contemplation, namely, his admiration for psychoanalysis. In psychoanalytic terms, a failure of acknowledgment can be further characterized as *a refusal* of acknowledgment: we repress the need to acknowledge the other. A related danger is that anyone wanting to oppose Cavell's readings, in certain circumstances, could be accused of repressing a need to acknowledge them. Critics of psychoanalysis sometimes suffer a similar fate.

27. Ibid., p. 194.

The point is not to deny the relevance of psychoanalysis in specific cases but to question the generality of its claims. This was Wittgenstein's point when he said that if we are to learn from psychoanalysis, it must be viewed *critically*.[28] It must be seen as *a* way of looking at certain matters. But in some cases, applying it will lead to distortion. For example, as a literary case take Flannery O'Connor's creation Mrs. Turpin in *Revelation*. She is a pharisaical person who 'comes to herself' as the result of a neurotic girl telling her to go back to hell and calling her a warthog. One might say that she is told what she needs to hear. But it does not follow at all that her pharisaism is an unconscious need to resist acknowledging that she is a sinner. As Rush Rhees argued, if this were so, her pharisaism gave her what she needed! As Rhees points out, "'She was told what she *needed* to hear' is a moral judgement, and cannot be understood in any other way. Reference to unconscious desires or repression has no purchase in this context."[29]

The parameters of Cavell's discussion can allow for flexibility of circumstances. In the case of artifacts, say, cutlery, Wittgenstein argues that we do not see the cutlery *as* cutlery. But with human beings, things are different. We are responsible for the ways we see them. But there is no 'best case' of such 'seeing'. Cavell says that we are engaged on the endless task of putting the limits of our present acknowledgments to the test of new situations. But despite these differences, Cavell sees an analogy between skepticism about the external world and skepticism concerning other minds. The skeptic denies that we see a physical object by invoking our ignorance of whichever side we are not seeing in perception. Similarly, because we cannot produce a best case for knowing the other, it is denied that we know the other at all. The skeptic would be satisfied only with something unreal, a perspective on an object or a human being that would not be any perspective in particular. The skeptic looks for the fixed perspective of a metaphysic that denies the world's flexibility. But this appeal to 'flexibility' may hide the quasi-psychoanalytic parameters of acknowledgment within which Cavell places his discussion.

For example, what of the religious categories necessary to understand Flannery O'Connor's story? In an early essay on Kierkegaard,

28. Ludwig Wittgenstein, "Conversations on Freud," in *Lectures on Aesthetics, Psychology, and Religious Belief*, ed. C. Barrett (Oxford: Blackwell, 1966).

29. Rush Rhees, "Self Deception and Needs," in *Moral Questions*, ed. D. Z. Phillips (London: Macmillan, 1999).

Cavell insists that religious dogmas must bear their own weight, be understood in their own terms, but this point of view changes in his later work.[30] He now advocates the categories of psychoanalysis for our understanding because, since the time of Descartes and Shakespeare, we have witnessed the fall of kings, the rise of the new science, and the death of God. No doubt religion has been affected in many ways by these changes, but for whom is Cavell speaking when he speaks of the death of God? He is no longer contemplating diverse possibilities.

Furthermore, he confuses possibilities. He runs together religious notions of transcendence with the distortions of them in metaphysical theories of transcendence, assuming that mortification of the flesh is equivalent to its denial. Similarly, in discussing Hollywood comedies of remarriage that Cavell sees as examples of overcoming skepticism through reacknowledgment, he does not consider possibilities in which these problems would be seen differently.[31] For example, reciprocity plays an important part in Cavell's notion of mutual acknowledgment in personal relationships. But what of cases in which love is not pointless simply because it is unrequited or has ceased to be reciprocated? It may be said that people probably cannot live with these difficulties, but for some, religious vows will determine how that difficulty is thought of in the first place. Cavell says that religious vows cannot guarantee marital relationships, but notoriously, neither can efforts at acknowledgment. Sometimes, at least, religion may be more realistic than the optimism in some therapeutic alternatives. But there will be situations where the opposite is the case. What I am insisting on is a philosophical contemplation of these diverse reactions without imposing a false unity on them.

Similar considerations apply to Cavell's treatment of Thoreau and Emerson in American culture.[32] He says that their lessons are what the culture needs most. If that is a moral or political claim on Cavell's part, he is perfectly entitled to it. It could be argued, however, that this claim is of a special kind, because Emersonian perfectionism enjoins us to imagine what is best, while leaving the final decision of *what* is best to our own judgment. It simply demands the contemplation of alternative possibilities, the imagining of other lives for ourselves, and is thus not

30. Stanley Cavell, "Kierkegaard's *On Authority and Revelation*," in *Must We Mean What We Say?*

31. Stanley Cavell, *Pursuits of Happiness* (Cambridge: Harvard University Press, 1981).

32. For example, Cavell, *Senses of Walden*.

the advocacy of a particular perspective. I think such a defense is illusory. First, it ignores the fact that this *kind* of openness is itself characteristic of a certain perspective, because what marks people off morally from one another is precisely what they are prepared to consider *as* alternatives. In Chapter 7 in discussing Martha Nussbaum, I shall emphasize again that this openness is not to be equated with the openness of philosophical contemplation. Second, the defense ignores Cavell's claims that our very rejection of the examples offered by Thoreau and Emerson is evidence that they are repressed in us. In this way, Cavell's thesis becomes self-authenticating.

Alternatively, it might be argued that Cavell knows full well what he is doing; is aware that it gets in the way, or could get in the way, of a contemplative conception of philosophy, blinding us to other possibilities; but thinks that the risk is worth it. I would reply that it is not a matter of risks but of what motivates one's investigation. Such a strategy, if ascribed to Cavell, would simply be different from the philosophical contemplation I discuss.

Furthermore, philosophical contemplation will embrace those opposed to the kind of Emersonian ideal about which Cavell talks. Wittgenstein's insistence in his discussion of ethics with Rhees is relevant here: other people's reasons in opposition to this ideal really are their reasons. Similarly, our rejection of ideas really can be a rejection of them and not a repressed fear of being tested by them. What would have been instructive and a furtherance of philosophical contemplation is a comparison of favorable views of Emersonian perfectionism with voices in American culture that were critical of it. For example, Flannery O'Connor said "that when Emerson decided in 1832 that he could no longer celebrate the Lord's supper unless the bread and wine were removed that an important step in the vaporization of religion in America had taken place."[33] Philosophical contemplation would be interested in the *kind* of disagreement this is. *Must* one view be shown to be confused? In this respect it would be instructive to contrast Wittgenstein's discussions of religion with Cavell's treatment of it. Cavell seems to be searching for postreligious alternatives for understanding our lives, whereas Wittgenstein, contemplating different modes of understanding, wonders at the fact that life can be like that. One offers the

33. Flannery O'Connor, *The Habit of Being*, ed. Sally Fitzgerald (New York: Farrar, Straus, and Giroux, 1979), p. 511.

road he prefers to travel on and thinks we need to travel on; the other shows us the city with no main road.

Michael Weston contends that, despite their antimetaphysical arguments, Nietzsche, Heidegger, and Derrida cannot resist replacing the metaphysics they attack with a *general* perspective of their own.[34] The question has been whether Cavell falls to the same temptation.

If the temptation were avoided, Cavell's *main* philosophical achievement would still be the light he throws on the struggle against skepticism. In the realm of values, aesthetic, moral, political, and religious differences would be recognized, along with their different attitudes to one another. Philosophical contemplation owes these differences the respect of recognition. But this recognition keeps the distinction between philosophical appreciation and personal appropriation.

These differences have their place in the hubbub of voices that make up human conversations, discussions in which different things bear on one another and which in turn bear on other conversations. This is the kind of unity that discourse has. The desire to go beyond the philosophical contemplation of such discourse is one of the major obstacles to the reception of Wittgenstein's thought—a failure of philosophical acknowledgment, one might say.

34. Michael Weston, *Kierkegaard and Modern Continental Philosophy* (London: Routledge, 1994).

6

Annette Baier and Moral Philosophy: "The Arrogance of Solitary Intellect"?

I t may seem that in arguing for the possibility of a contemplative conception of philosophy, I seek to restore a conception of philosophical neutrality thought to be long out of fashion. In this chapter I shall explore this reaction in the context of contemporary moral philosophy.

What is it for moral philosophy to be neutral? In his editorial foreword to P. H. Nowell-Smith's *Ethics*, published in 1954, A. J. Ayer wrote, "There is a distinction ... between the activity of the moralist ... and that of a moral philosopher."[1] Cora Diamond comments:

> For Ayer that distinction was a straightforward one. The moral philosopher as such makes no moral judgements; the moralist, on the other hand, 'sets out to elaborate a moral code, or to encourage its observance.' Thus Ayer went on to describe Nowell-Smith as a moral philosopher: he 'shows how ethical statements are related to, and how they differ from, statements of other types, and what are the criteria appropriate to them.' Ayer's idea was that this could be done without the philosopher's taking sides on any moral or practical issue. For Ayer, then, three things were closely linked: the distinction between moralist and moral philosopher, the ethical neutrality of the philosopher, the characterization of his own aim as linguistic or conceptual clarification.[2]

But was this conception of neutrality maintained, even when it was in fashion? In the very book, *Ethics*, said to manifest moral neutrality,

1. A. J. Ayer, foreword to *Ethics*, by P. H. Nowell-Smith (Harmondsworth: Penguin, 1954), p. 7.
2. Cora Diamond, "Having a Rough Story about What Moral Philosophy Is," in *The Realistic Spirit* (Cambridge: MIT Press, 1991), p. 367.

Nowell-Smith writes: "Moral philosophy is a practical science; its aim is to answer questions in the form 'What shall I do?'" To help us answer this question, what it does is to "paint a picture of various types of life in the manner of Plato and ask which type of life you really want to lead."[3]

Whatever one's opinion of this conception of philosophy's task, Diamond is in no doubt that "it has now gone out of fashion to hold that the moral philosopher as such makes no moral judgements." Further, "going along with fashion ... we give up ethical neutrality, and recognize it to be neither desirable nor indeed possible. With it, we drop the idea that the aim of moral philosophy is limited to conceptual clarification."[4] We have seen in previous chapters that a contemplative conception of philosophy goes beyond a view of philosophy as limited to conceptual clarification. The latter notion is consistent, for example, with an underlaborer conception of philosophy, which at this stage is of little consequence, because the contemplative conception is even more out of fashion in our technological culture.

Discussing why something goes out of fashion in philosophy would be a mixed and tangled business, but on one thing we must surely agree: it would be philosophically irresponsible and culpable to give up a view or to embrace one on the grounds that it was fashionable to do so. So instead of following fashion, let us ask whether it is premature of Diamond to describe "the notion of neutral analysis of moral terms" as "dead or moribund."[5]

Much will depend on what we mean by the neutrality of moral philosophy. Part of what Diamond has in mind is the attempt to account for moral concepts in purely formal terms, independently of their actual content and the role they play in human life. Moral neutrality in moral philosophy may also be a claim for it as a neutral arbiter between conflicting moral views, bringing an ordered priority to the chaos of our disagreements and differences. These conceptions of neutrality are indeed confused, but I shall not argue that case here.[6]

But is this all that neutrality can mean? I contend that there is a neutrality connected with a contemplative conception of philosophy. It

3. Quoted by Diamond in ibid., pp. 367–68.
4. Ibid., p. 380.
5. Ibid.
6. I have done so in many of the essays to be found in *Interventions in Ethics* (London: Macmillan; Albany: State University of New York Press, 1992).

comes from puzzles about the possibility of morality. What is it to have a moral conviction? What does disagreement come to in morality? Conceptual recognition of the heterogeneity of morals grows out of reflection on these matters, and it goes with wonder at the fact that people do have the moral problems that they do, what they take to be difficulties, the disagreements they have, and the diverse ways in which all these enter their lives.

In the argument for a contemplative conception of philosophy, an intriguing intellectual fact emerges. Those who think that moral neutrality in moral philosophy is dead ignore the tradition to which this conception belongs. This tradition shares their criticisms of neutrality, without abandoning the concept of neutrality altogether. It agrees that no purely formal account of moral concepts is satisfactory. But it also denies, unlike the recent opponents of neutrality, that moral philosophy, aided or unaided, can tell us how we ought to live. *In clinging to this idea, the recent opponents of neutrality turn out not to be neutral after all, while claiming that a refined form of reflection should inform, at least, the general direction of the good life.* But this latter claim is characteristic of a confused notion of neutrality. Thus the distinction between the moral philosopher and the moralist is blurred further.

It may be said that in this and the following chapter, *I am trying to rescue neutrality from distortions of itself.* In doing so, a contemplative conception of philosophy is rescued at the same time.

As we have seen, Wittgenstein alludes to a contemplative conception of philosophy in *Culture and Value* when he says: "My ideal is a certain coolness. A temple providing a setting for the passions without meddling with them."[7] Annette Baier, by contrast, is a moral philosopher in a panic, worried about the effect the teaching of moral philosophy is having on our students: "We, in effect, give courses in comparative ethical theory, and like courses in comparative religion, their usual effect on the student is loss of faith in *any* of the alternatives presented. We produce relativists and moral skeptics, persons who have been convinced by our teaching that whatever they do in some difficult situation, some moral theory will condone it, another will condemn it." This, of course, was not the intention of the teachers: "Most of us do not aim to produce moral skeptics when we teach introductory ethics.

7. Ludwig Wittgenstein, *Culture and Value,* ed. G. H. von Wright, trans. Peter Winch (Oxford: Blackwell, 1980), p. 2e.

But that is what we do with most of our students, when we teach moral theories and their application to cases."[8]

We may be tempted not to take these budding moral skeptics too seriously, claiming that their behavior shows that they believe what their skepticism denies. Baier seems to have had worse luck, for she claims that the philosophical instruction has led to actual moral disasters: "What we aim to do is increase reflective awareness of what is at stake in difficult decisions, to produce more thoughtful, better informed, and presumably wiser people. The best reason to believe that there is something amiss with the whole procedure is that it is defeating its own ends. In attempting to increase moral reflectiveness we may be destroying what conscience there once was in those we teach."[9] What am I being asked to believe here—that the products of the introductory ethics classes have had what little conscience they once had destroyed? How do they behave when the classes are over—without any trace of conscience? Do they lie with impunity, betray friends whenever they feel like it, steal what they want, and murder when pushed? These really would be terrifying products of introductory ethics classes. Pity the poor teachers: wanting to produce moral characters, they seem to have produced monsters.

How is all this supposed to have come about? Apparently, the students had something before the rot set in: "Such moral convictions as people have before studying moral philosophy were not acquired by self-conscious acceptance of a theory. Most parents lack the intellectualist's compulsion to transform their moral beliefs into theories. What they pass on to their children may be a few slogans or principles or commandments, but mainly they impart moral constraints by example and by reaction to behaviour, not by handing on explicit verbal codes of general rules, let alone moral theories."[10] G. E. M. Anscombe has commented on this feature of early moral training and the role within it of what she calls 'stopping modals', where the child is told that she or he *must* do this and *cannot* do that. These 'stopping modals' are accompanied by reasons that Anscombe calls the *logos* of the modals. It is a feature of these reasons that their force is bound up with the modals in such a way that evoking them is sufficient to justify restraining the

8. Annette Baier, "Theory and Reflective Practices," in *Postures of the Mind* (London: Methuen, 1985), pp. 207–8, 208.

9. Ibid.

10. Ibid.

child's behavior: "You mustn't do that, it hurts," "You must go, you promised," "You can't go there, it's private," and so on.[11] What we have here are early moral interventions in the life of a family that have varying degrees of success. They will not be effective if the child never gets beyond seeing them in terms of sanctions and rewards, but through these interventions the child may come to have a regard for truthfulness, fairness, recognition of privacy, condemnation of privacy, and so on.

Moral philosophers, as Baier points out, insist on seeing theories behind this moral training; they reduce traditions to rules, and rules to theories. Thus to the multiplicity of traditions and contexts in which children receive moral training is added a multiplicity of moral theories. Chaos results: "In a pluralistic society like this one there is no escaping the fact that there are a plurality of moral traditions, that what people learn at their parents' knees varies from one ethnic or religious group to another. This substantive moral disagreement is a fact that no reforms in the teaching of introductory ethics will conjure away. Catholic hospitals will make different decisions from non-Catholic hospitals on many cases, whatever we philosophers do in our classes.... The array of moral theories that philosophers have produced does not match the array of working moral traditions in this society, or in the world at large."[12] The result, according to Baier, is that we lose our moral bearings: "So we might expect to end up with Catholic utilitarians, Catholic contractarians, Catholic intuitionists; Protestant variants of all these; atheist variants of all these. In fact the alternatives tend to cancel one another out, leaving a moral vacuum." Baier's pessimistic conclusion is, "A better recipe for moral cynicism could scarcely be deliberately devised."[13]

It is clear from Baier's remarks that not only does she think the philosophy students are thoroughly confused by their teachers, but that the teachers themselves, the providers of moral theories, are equally confused. She is hardly the first in this century not simply to criticize one theory in the name of another but also to have doubts about the very conception of a moral theory. Thirty-five years ago, J. L. Stocks noted of the relation between moral theories and the heterogeneity of

11. See G. E. M. Anscombe, "Rules, Rights, and Promises," in *Collected Philosophical Papers*, vol. 3 (Oxford: Blackwell, 1981).

12. Baier, "Theory and Reflective Practices," pp. 208–9.

13. Ibid., p. 209.

morals that "there is obviously an enormous gap between this chaotic material and the tidy ethical systems which philosophers offer us as a result of their reflections upon it. The philosopher does not trouble much to show the steps by which from that starting point he arrived at this result. It often seems as though he had been content to generalise from his own limited experience assuming that it was typical or authoritative."[14] Little attention was paid to Stocks's caution in 1931, as the history of subsequent ethical theory testifies.

Where does this leave us, as philosophers, with regard to moral theories, theories that are supposed to guide us in our conduct? Diamond says: "No one knows what the subject is; most widely agreed accounts of it depend on suppositions that are not obvious and that reflect particular evaluations and views of the world, of human nature, and of what it is to speak, think, write or read about the world."[15] Rules about what is to count as moral philosophy or moral theory turn out to be useless, because every time they are laid down, two consequences follow.

First, when examples are produced that clearly fall outside the proposed theory, the theorist will resort to desperate measures to accommodate them. Georges Sorel has drawn attention to this tendency: "The philosophers always have a certain amount of difficulty in seeing clearly into these ethical problems, because they feel the impossibility of harmonising the ideas which are current at a given time in a class, and yet imagine it to be their duty to reduce everything to a unity. To conceal from themselves the fundamental heterogeneity of all this civilised morality, they have recourse to a great number of subterfuges, sometimes relegating to the rank of exceptions, importations, or survivals, everything which embarrasses them."[16]

Second, if someone lays down rules for what moral philosophy *must* be, another person will simply go ahead and break the rules. Thus, speaking of Martha Nussbaum's work, Diamond states, "By thinking philosophically about literature in a way that breaks the rules of what counts—on many views—as moral philosophy, she goes some way toward showing that we should not take those rules seriously."[17]

14. J. L. Stocks, "Can Philosophy Determine What Is Ethically or Socially Valuable?" in J. L. Stocks, *Morality and Purpose*, ed. with an introduction by D. Z. Phillips (London: Routledge, 1970), p. 124.

15. Diamond, "Moral Philosophy," p. 380.

16. Georges Sorel, *Reflections on Violence*, trans. T. E. Hulme (London: Collier, 1961), pp. 229–30.

17. Diamond, "Moral Philosophy," p. 380.

Are we to conclude from this picture of confused students being guided by confused theories that no one knows what moral philosophy is or that the notion of such a subject is itself a confused one? No, that conclusion should not be drawn. Diamond thinks that the rule-governed moral philosophy she attacks is confused. She reaches this conclusion through discussion, a discussion that simply has to continue. Often, obstacles in philosophical discussion are not obstacles of the intellect but of the will; we do not want to give up a certain way of thinking. It is in giving up the hold of these tendencies, according to Wittgenstein, that we *suffer* in doing philosophy. We feel that we cannot give up the view that moral philosophy should guide our conduct. We feel ashamed if we say we should do this, because it seems to be a loss of vocation and an expression of loss of confidence in our subject. Yet I want to argue that to cling to the idea that moral philosophy has the task of telling us what the moral character of our lives should be is itself to display a lack of character, and in the remainder of the chapter I attempt to justify this claim. I begin by showing that even when the theoretical aspirations of moral philosophy have been put aside, the aim of determining our moral conduct—or the nature of the good life—remains with many philosophers. In considering two examples, I will, at the same time, illustrate a contemplative conception of philosophy.

J. L. Stocks, having noted the gap between the tidiness of ethical theories and the heterogeneity of moral judgments and deliberations, says that the would-be theorist of moral conduct still has a task to perform, namely, to reduce the chaotic material that faces him or her to some kind of order: "He has to show that this multiplicity is at bottom a unity, that this unorganized sequence of decisions and judgements has none the less its own inner organisation and can be plausibly regarded as the expression of a single principle or a few fundamental ideas which are in intelligible relation to one another."[18] Stocks avoids the accusation that he is imposing a unity on our moral practices, because he claims that the moral philosopher is simply making explicit the principles implicit in them. In this way people can be reminded of principles they are apt to forget in the busy press of life. The difficulty for Stocks is that he cannot avoid Baier's correct observation that these practices are diverse and that principles at work in them will be equally diverse. As she says, no introductory course in ethics can explain this diversity away.

18. Stocks, "What Is Ethically or Socially Valuable?" p. 125.

Yet my second example concerns Baier herself. Having come to her conclusions, she cannot give up the conception of moral philosophy as a guide to human conduct. She asks whether her conclusion means "that we should live by our inherited fuzzy moral intuitions and do no moral philosophy at all."[19] Baier thinks that many great philosophers offer us an alternative. They do not offer us complete moral systems that claim to be perfect but ask us to reflect on our moral perspectives to see whether they can be improved. This reflection contributes to more successful coexistence. Baier does not believe enough effort has been made in this direction, calling it "one version of the enlightenment project [which] has not yet been given a fair enough trial for us to know whether it will or will not fail— ... Hume's attempt to give morality a secure basis not in moral theory, but in human capacities for cooperation."[20]

Baier assumes, uncritically, that moral instruction to children *must* be fuzzy, but I see no reason for thinking so. It may turn out to be a touchstone for life. Perhaps it was such a touchstone that enabled Flannery O'Connor to say, "When in Rome, do as you done in Milledgeville."[21] For Baier, while the values into which a child is initiated do not await a theory, they do stand in need of a reflective rationale. I certainly do not want to deny that a moral perspective may deepen or change as the result of reflection. Reflection is called for not only when conflicting values are encountered, values different from those of one's early years, but also when moral dilemmas are created by the very values one has acquired. But such possibilities retain the heterogeneity that Baier finds problematic. She is not content to remain, philosophically, with the different ways in which moral character may be expressed when different values clash or when our own values create dilemmas. This is because her idea of a rationale is foundationalist, although not theoretical. Although expressed with caution, her underlying position is that reflection should lead us to the view that the worthwhile values are those which facilitate cooperation between us.

Baier holds that reflection may show confusions in the rationales we give of our values. I am saying that the philosophical rationale Baier offers is confused. For anyone with serious moral values, it will not be

19. Baier, "Theory and Reflective Practices," p. 224.
20. Baier, "Doing without Moral Theory?" in *Postures of the Mind*, pp. 230–31.
21. Flannery O'Connor, *The Habit of Being*, ed. Sally Fitzgerald (New York: Vintage Books, 1980).

the conditions of cooperation with others that determine whether co-operation is possible. Limitations in the circumstances may make a measure of cooperation unavoidable, in which case it will be *a* value in the situation, but not necessarily the value of greatest importance. It may be tolerated because it safeguards values thought to be of far greater importance than itself. We saw this in Chapter 4 in discussing Rorty's notion of a hermeneutic conversation. So for all the recent discussions of a 'reflective equilibrium', we might well remind ourselves that it may be anything but benign to suggest that diverse moral views *must* be subordinated to a cooperative ideal. Everything depends on the moral character of the cooperation.

It is said, sometimes, that 'society' cannot 'go on' if deeply different moral perspective exist, an argument that has always puzzled me because that is precisely how it does go on. Think of an academic community as a small-scale example. Is it not true that within any academic community, even one established by a single vision, we find different points of view concerning, say, the ideals of a university or of education more generally, different values, different priorities? Within that community there may be, and usually is, a rhetoric which says that it cannot go on without a common view, whereas, as we all know, it actually does go on without one.

Although Baier's cooperative ideal is not itself a theory, she is not averse to using theories to find out what values actually facilitate such cooperation. She regards the variety of moral views that no moral theory captures as experiments in living. To see whether these experiments work we need, apparently, the help of many nonphilosophical theories: "We need psychological theories and social theories, and, if we are intent on political change, theories about political power and its working and about economies. But do we need *normative* theories, theories to tell us what to do, in addition to theories that present to us the world in which we are to try to do it?" Baier has no doubt that we do. She has nothing but disdain for a division of labor "in which the theorists keep their hands clean of real-world applications, and the ones who advise the decision-makers, those who do 'applied ethics.' "[22] She asks, "Does the profession of moral philosophy now display that degeneration of a Kantian moral outlook that Hegel portrays, where there are beautiful souls doing their theoretical thing and averting their eyes

22. Baier, "Doing without Moral Theory?" p. 235.

from what is happening in the real world, even from what is happening in the way of 'application' of their own theories, and there are those who are paid to be the 'conscience' of the medical business or legal profession, what Hegel calls the moral *valets*, the professional moral judges?" The moral guides we adopt, according to Baier, must be determined socially and historically. She claims that "unless we know the fate of communities that tried to implant and live by the moral principles we consider, how can we have any empirically tested opinion about their soundness?"[23] It seems that such an experiment takes generations to perform, and I have asked what we are supposed to be doing in the meantime.[24] But this does not get to the heart of the problem.

The fundamental assumption in Baier which must be questioned is that moral philosophy is a guide to human conduct. With the increasing call for applied ethics, Baier predicts more and more cooperation between philosophy and other disciplines in the search for moral answers. It seems that we must abandon any *distinctive* philosophical task for ethics. The merger with other disciplines, Baier argues, "might help us to escape from that arrogance of solitary intellect which has condemned much moral theory to sustained self-delusions concerning its subject matter, its methods, and its authority."[25]

Here we see a powerful example of how a conception of morality as a guide to conduct influences Baier's conclusion that moral philosophy too, aided by other disciplines, must be such a guide. I hope to show that what leads Baier to accuse moral philosophy of an "arrogance of solitary intellect" is a loss of a certain sense of what a philosophical problem can be, one connected with a contemplative view of the subject. Thus, far from this leading to a conception of "beautiful souls doing their theoretical thing" and averting their eyes from the practitioners of "applied ethics," it may lead to the much needed recognition that, despite its name, "applied ethics" need not be a search for answers but a philosophical contemplation of possibilities of moral sense in certain contexts in our lives.

We can begin to see that moral philosophy is not a guide to human conduct by realizing that morality itself is not such a guide. How does

---

23. Ibid., pp. 236, 242.

24. See my "What Can We Expect from Ethics?" in *Interventions in Ethics,* where I criticize the notion of 'experiments' in living and the comparable conception in Bernard Williams, *Ethics and the Limits of Philosophy* (Cambridge: Harvard University Press, 1985).

25. Baier, "Doing without Moral Theory?" p. 244.

the notion that morality is a guide to conduct come about? Peter Winch has shown that it is influenced by a caricature of our relation to the world at work in much of moral philosophy, a caricature that philosophers would deny if it were put to them: "The picture of the agent involved here is, as it were, of a spectator of a world which includes his own body; though this spectator is also able, to a limited extent, to effect changes in the world he observes. So he needs to be presented with considerations which will show him why he should initiate one set of physical changes rather than another, or rather than none at all; he needs guidance, that is, in the exercise of his will. Morality is thought by many philosophers as one such guide."[26] Winch is not denying the phenomenon of moral guidance but the account given by philosophers of the context in which need for such guidance arises, a context in which it is said a person has certain goals he or she wants to achieve and certain obstacles stand in the way of achieving them, obstacles such as lack of money, lack of natural ability, lack of friends, and so on. The guide the person needs should then help him or her to overcome these obstacles and to get what he or she wants. Yet, as Winch points out, morality seems to have little to do with removing such obstacles:

> On the contrary, were it not for morality, they would often be a great deal easier to overcome. What are the difficulties, then, which morality can show us the way round? I do not know what answers can be given except to say they are moral difficulties. For instance, a man devotes himself to building up a business and then finds that the whole enterprise will founder if he does not do something morally questionable—something perhaps that does not amount to legal fraud, and involves him in no risk of suffering ill repute among his fellows, but something nevertheless which he regards as morally inadmissible. Morality, we are told, is a guide which helps him round his difficulty. But were it not for morality, there would be no difficulty! This is a strange sort of guide, which first puts obstacles in our path and then shows us the way round them. Would it not be far simpler and more rational to be shot of the thing altogether? Then we could get on with the matter in hand, whatever it is.[27]

In contrast to this account that I, like Winch, claim to be a caricature of moral concern, we can see that moral considerations, for the

26. Peter Winch, "Moral Integrity," in *Ethics and Action* (London: Routledge, 1972), pp. 171–72.
27. Ibid., pp. 172–73.

moral agent, are *constitutive* of what individuals take the situation, including the alternatives facing them, to be. Their moral character, or lack of it, will determine what they think is open to them or not. That character is not itself an end of their actions. It is something which may or may not show *in* their actions.

I have referred elsewhere to a television debate I saw on abortion between a "scientific rationalist" and a Roman Catholic woman.[28] She was expecting a child and was already the mother of others. She had been told that there were dangers involved in her forthcoming pregnancy. She insisted that were it to become a matter of choice between her life and that of the child she was carrying, her own should be sacrificed. The rationalist was appalled and emphasized her responsibility to her other children, what her death would mean to her husband, the economic implications for the family, the rights of the born as against those of the unborn, and so on. He seemed to think that she did not understand these considerations, which for him constituted 'our rational wants' and to which her religious convictions were obstacles. She, on the other hand, stressed that she was fully aware of the difficulties mentioned but said that the privilege of bringing a child into the world was a grace she could not refuse and that a life could not be sacrificed in the way the rationalist proposed. It is far more likely that she understood what he meant by the dangers he enumerated, than that he understood what she meant by a grace bestowed on her by God. While he insisted that he was appealing to 'what we all want', she wanted other things. But she did not believe in her values because she had these wants. Rather, she had these wants because she believed. The rationalist insisted that she had no choice, given the dangers, to sacrifice her child. She insisted that she had no choice but to sacrifice her own life. Unless one appreciates how moral or religious considerations are constitutive of the situations facing us, one will not do justice to the ways in which these real moral differences occur.

But the differences between the rationalist and the Roman Catholic mother may simply reinforce the view that such disagreements are 'incomplete' and await a resolution by moral theory. The universalizability thesis was meant to serve just that function, for it held that for a moral view to be such, it must be one that everyone would hold in the same situation. Thus the disagreement between the

28. See "On Morality's Having a Point" (with H. O. Mounce) in *Interventions in Ethics*, pp. 11–12.

rationalist and the mother cannot be allowed to remain unresolved philosophically. In relation to one's own moral beliefs, the universalizability thesis is saying something important. If there were no consistency in a person's moral judgments from one day to the next, we would not know where he or she stands morally or even what he or she was saying. It does not follow, however, that I must say that if I have a moral opinion, everyone else, in the same circumstances, must hold the same opinion. I may say, in disputes over abortion, for example, that others, with whom I disagree, did what was right for them. Decisions concerning divorce would be another example. The phrase 'right for them' may lead to fears of Protagorean relativism: that I am saying that whatever people say is right, is right. Winch has shown that this fear is misplaced if the situation in which people reach their decisions has certain features. First, it must be clear that moral considerations have led to their conclusion and that not anything can count as such considerations. Second, their decision must be free from self-deception. Third, Winch recognizes that the kind of decision arrived at must be one not too far removed from what I am prepared to call 'moral' and that people will vary morally and psychologically in this respect. It is important to note that Winch is not advocating the response "They did what was right for them" or saying that one cannot call the others' decisions right or wrong. He *is* saying that "They did what was right for them" is *also* a moral response and that its possibility should not be ruled out philosophically.

R. M. Hare is sensitive to the crassness that may result from certain applications of the universalizability thesis: "Since we cannot know everything about another person's concrete situation (including how it strikes him, which may make all the difference), it is nearly always presumptuous to suppose that another person's situation is exactly like we have ourselves been in, or even like it in relevant particulars."[29] Winch replies by asking what the difference is between people in disagreements of the kind I have mentioned: "If we want to *express,* in a given situation, how it strikes the agent, we cannot dispense with his inclination to come to a particular moral decision.... But what did [their] difference consist in? Surely in the fact that, faced with two conflicting sets of considerations, the one ... was disposed to give precedence to the one ... the other to give precedence to the other.... If such dispositions as this have to be taken into account in applying the notion of

29. R. M. Hare, *Freedom and Reason* (Oxford: Clarendon Press, 1963), p. 49.

'exactly the same circumstances,' surely the last vestige of logical force is removed from the universalizability thesis."[30]

Furthermore, how could there be a 'moral resolution' of any issue that did not include such dispositions? To want to go beyond them is to ignore the very character of *moral* disagreements. Philosophy should allow them to be themselves and not regard them as 'incomplete' or awaiting resolution in a wider 'reflective' equilibrium. It is sometimes thought that this view is a denial of reflection or change of view, but this is not so. What must be noted is that such changes come about, sometimes because inconsistencies in one's values are pointed out or because other values one comes to appreciate erode one's former allegiances. But this erosion, so far from being independent of moral judgments, would be unintelligible without them. Here, I am simply going to give several examples from Rush Rhees's writings about how *some* examples may go. He took part in a debate on euthanasia where, as usual, the motion was phrased in general terms: "This House believes ..." Rhees thought the issue could not be discussed in *that* way and tried to confine attention to a view he thought difficult to maintain, namely, that euthanasia is *never* justified in any circumstances. For example suppose someone says that it would interfere with the will of God. Rhees replies:

> I will say only that there are certain cases in which I would *not* say it was wrong for a doctor to take measures to prolong a patient's life; and similarly that there are cases in which I would not condemn either the patient who takes his life or the persons who make it possible for him to do so. There are circumstances in which I cannot hope that an invalid will recover. 'There is brain damage. There is a blood clot again. If he does recover his intelligence (and his speech) will probably be affected.' No one closely connected with him hopes that he will recover to that sort of life. He has been impoverished enough already. Suppose I had a proper sense of the sacredness of life—would a sense of the sacredness of life make me wish that he may live in those circumstances? If I were religious, would I pray for his recovery or pray for his death? Would a proper sense of the sacredness of life make me hope that the doctor will omit nothing in his efforts to keep him alive? Would there not be something *un*holy in using highly developed skills and drugs to prolong life in that form? Would there not be something wrong with that sense of medical responsibility?[31]

30. Winch, "The Universalizability of Moral Judgements," in *Ethics and Action,* p. 169.
31. Rush Rhees, "Euthanasia," in *Moral Questions,* ed. D. Z. Phillips (London: Macmillan, 1999).

On the other hand, Rhees is also opposed to the medical view that regards "life [as] something between birth and death [where] both of these are delegated to hospitals, shut off from the access of unauthorized persons. And none but a peeping tom would try to find out what happens.... 'There is nothing to wonder at in the fact that we exist. It is all part of a social policy.' 'Death is just an irreparable misfortune. But we can do a great deal to control it when it comes.' ... The thought of death may be present repeatedly in your decisions; raising the question whether it is not futile, whether understanding anything at all is not futile. To recognize the majesty of death is to recognize the difficulties and the puzzles which there are in life." Rhees notes: "Much may depend on the attitude towards life and death on the part of the invalid and also on the part of the person who might make death possible. The profanation or the blasphemy or the irreverence will depend largely on what these people think." Different people will arrive at different conclusions: "One might decide: 'However terrible the dying, I cannot do anything to make it shorter.' And I would never blame him or say that he was wrong. But neither would I blame the one who said it were [*sic*] better to lessen the horror and that his love for the dying person demanded this." I do not think Rhees means to deny that others would criticize where he would not. Speaking for himself, he says: "If a man wanted to die, and if I had no doubt of this; and if he was afraid to take his own life and asked me to kill him—I should refuse to do so, I think. This would be partly from a primitive horror."[32]

These remarks hardly convey how much there is in Rhees's discussion of this issue. My main purpose in quoting them is hopefully to convey something of what he takes moral reflection to be. It is not a general theorizing about such matters. Of course, the people reflecting are trying to decide what to do and how to think about the situation. But Rhees's purpose is to give us a sense of the kind of issue they are facing, not to settle it for us. If we have appreciated what he has to say, we can see why moral philosophy cannot do *that*.

Onora O'Neill criticizes what she sees as a Wittgensteinian tradition for failing to embrace this task.[33] In response, I said: "O'Neill has a conception of moral philosophy as a guide to human conduct. She never comes to grips with the fact that Winch is challenging that conception.

32. Ibid.
33. Onora O'Neill, "The Power of Example," in *Constructions of Reason* (Cambridge: Cambridge University Press, 1989).

For her, he is simply seen as someone whose examples lack the power to give us the moral guidance we need. O'Neill fails to appreciate that Winch is not offering examples which *await* our moral judgements. He is presenting examples of people making moral judgements. Winch wants us to note the complexity involved in these judgements" and, in that way, to contemplate what they come to.[34]

Baier says that she learned from Wittgenstein's *Brown Book* not to turn every rule into a theory. But she did not learn that Wittgenstein, as Rhees says, "would constantly describe 'different ways of doing it,' but he did not call them different ways of doing the same thing.... He did not see them as so many fumbling attempts to say what none of them ever does say perfectly. The variety is important—not in order to fix your gaze on the unadulterated form, but to keep you from looking for it."[35] What I mean by the neutrality of philosophy, a neutrality that fashion has abandoned at high cost, is the perspicuous representation and contemplation of this variety. But this representation subserves contemplation of what moral convictions are and is connected with wonder in philosophy:

> Wonder that there should be the problems that there are, and that they should have the solutions that they do.... Trying to understand these questions—and from this angle or in this sense to understand human thinking and human investigation and human life; to understand how they rise in and in one sense belong to, our thinking about other questions that we ask and answer. This goes with *contemplation* of the ways in which people think and enquire—e.g. in trying to solve problems of physics, or in connexion with moral problems. And this is difficult. Perhaps especially so in a culture which has become as technological as our own—as much preoccupied with getting things done, with how to do things, with results.[36]

Philosophy's contemplative task is an ideal that is never fully realized, but it marks a direction in which our inquiries can travel toward "a setting for the passions without meddling with them."[37] This is not "the arrogance of solitary intellect" but rather philosophy's difficult, yet distinctive, contemplative task.

---

34. D. Z. Phillips, "The Presumption of Theory," in *Interventions in Ethics*, p. 70. This is a criticism of O'Neill's paper.

35. Rush Rhees, "Some Developments in Wittgenstein's View of Ethics," in *Discussions of Wittgenstein* (London: Routledge, 1970), p. 102.

36. Rush Rhees, "The Fundamental Problems of Philosophy," ed. Timothy Tessin, *Philosophical Investigations* 17, 4 (October 1994): 578–79.

37. Wittgenstein, *Culture and Value*, p. 2e.

7
Nussbaum on Ethics and Literature: A Cool Place for Characters?

Martha Nussbaum believes that moral theories have done a great deal of harm in moral philosophy. Whatever criticisms I make in this chapter, she has made an important contribution to the subject in showing that our moral concerns cannot be discussed adequately in terms of applying general principles to particular situations. I agree with these observations and have emphasized the ways we may misrepresent the role that rules do play in our lives: "We stare at moral and religious rules expecting them to have some kind of magical necessary effect on us, not realising that it is not the rules which give life to our lives, but our lives which give life to our rules."[1] Nussbaum thinks that moral philosophy has much to learn from literature, but it is important to appreciate the extent of the lesson she thinks needs to be learned by philosophers. Cora Diamond argues that it is not sufficient to treat literature as providing examples which will then be legitimated by some moral theory or another. It is not even enough, after reading a novel, say, one involving adultery and marriage, to see, as philosophers, "that our previous answers to those questions were inadequate, that we had failed to take into account certain human possibilities of what we can now see to be likelihoods, certain ways in which situations may be resolved or possible explanations for their being irresolvable, possible kinds of background or complications of character." If this were all, we would simply "modify or refine our general principles or our systematic account of how principles

---

1. D. Z. Phillips, "Following Rules," in *From Fantasy to Faith* (London: Macmillan, 1991), p. 72.

bear on cases." None of this pays sufficient attention to "*how* the story is told, the 'unplainess' of the telling, its 'density,' the kinds of demand that it makes on the reader."[2] For all the talk of linguistic philosophy, the trouble with most of the philosophers who practiced it was that they were guilty of what Iris Murdoch calls "a mistrust of language."[3] They emaciated the language of moral reflection in the generality of their terminology. By contrast, Nussbaum's philosophical attention to literature, according to Diamond, is "an attempt to connect features it has specifically as a novel with the character of what in human life the novel is about.... 'How is it that *this* (whatever feature of the novel it may be) is an illuminating way of writing about *that* (whatever feature of human life)?' ... [and] 'How is it that *this* is so much more illuminating a way of writing about it than are the familiar ways of moral philosophy?' "[4] If moral philosophy really appropriated these questions, it would abandon its dominant modes of argument and become acquainted with and give attention to these unplain, literary uses of language.

Clearly, Nussbaum's observations are meant to reveal the radical inadequacies of moral theory. But, as we saw in the last chapter, when philosophers abandon philosophical theories about morality, it does not follow that they abandon the conception of moral philosophy as a guide to conduct. That conception proves to be much harder to give up. This is the case with Nussbaum. She proclaims enthusiastically, "I have said that the question with which my projected literary-ethical inquiry begins is the question, 'How should one live?' "[5] She simply thinks the question is answered better by her mode of inquiry than by traditional moral theories. What is more, she believes that the task places a major responsibility on the moral philosopher but is one that she nevertheless finds exhilarating:

> These goals matter. Each of us is not only a professional, but a human being who is trying to live well; and not simply a human being, but also a citizen of some town, some country, above all a world of human be-

2. Cora Diamond, "Having a Rough Story about What Moral Philosophy Is," in *The Realistic Spirit* (Cambridge: MIT Press, 1991), p. 378.

3. Iris Murdoch, "Vision and Choice in Morality," *Proceedings of the Aristotelian Society* 30 (1956): 42 n.

4. Diamond, "Moral Philosophy," p. 379.

5. Martha Nussbaum, "Perceptive Equilibrium: Literary Theory and Ethical Theory," in *Love's Knowledge* (Oxford: Oxford University Press, 1990), p. 173.

ings, in which attunement and understanding are extremely urgent matters. Now certainly we can promote these goals in indefinitely many ways, apart from our professional lives: by raising children,[6] by engaging in some form of political action, by using money generously, by seeing and conversing and feeling. And yet, when a person happens to have a professional activity that is or becomes relevant to major ends of human life—how exhilarating that activity then is, and how deep, I think, the obligations it then imposes.[7]

If one thinks that the moral theories philosophers produce erode the richness of our moral vocabularies and the complexities of human relationships, a turn to literature may seem natural, for there one finds *diverse* portrayals of people's moral struggles and the equally diverse ways in which they resolve them or live with them. It may seem at first as though Nussbaum recognizes this diversity, but a closer examination shows that this is not so. It is for this reason, along with her "goals," that I do not think her work exemplifies a contemplative conception of philosophy.

This contention may seem unfair. It is easy to think so, because Nussbaum concentrates on examples that are meant to convey the openness of her inquiries. The examples show us that moral concerns and convictions are not safe affairs, immune from the contingencies of life. Maggie Verver, in Henry James's *The Golden Bowl*, wants her life to be like "a pure and perfect crystal, completely without crack or seam, both pervious and safely hard."[8] But Nussbaum brings out the price that the desire for such perfection exacts. It leads to the denial of her adult sexuality and to a failure to recognize or to accept other people for what they are. Maggie will not admit that values may clash. This, too, exacts its price: "Knowledge of a good, that is to say a value, in the world requires, we see, knowledge of evil, that is to say of the possibility of conflict, disorder, the contingent necessity of breaking or harming. Without eating the fruit she is just a child, ignorant of the value of the good as well." Nussbaum is saying that we must accept that the world in which we have to reflect and act, like the world of *The Golden Bowl*, is "a fallen world—a world, that is, in which innocence cannot be and is not

---

6. It would not occur to me to speak of raising children as a promotion of goals. The children are not *for* anything.

7. Nussbaum, "Perceptive Equilibrium," p. 192.

8. Martha Nussbaum, "Flawed Crystals: James's *The Golden Bowl* and Literature as Moral Philosophy," in *Love's Knowledge*, p. 125.

safely preserved, a world where values and loves are so pervasively in tension one with another that there is no safe human expectation of a perfect fidelity to all throughout a life."[9]

Nussbaum wants us to pursue James's ideal of becoming "finely aware and richly responsible," an ideal that can be pursued as long as it itself is not turned "into a new form of watertight purity." She claims "that a deep love may sometimes require an infidelity against even this adult spiritual standard." So any desire to know, in advance, where to draw the line is confused:

> When are we to pursue this ideal and when to let it go? How much is deep love worth, and under what circumstances is it worth a blinding? What boundaries are we to draw? What priorities can we fix? These, I take it, are the little girls' questions, resurfacing now, again, at yet another level—as they will resurface so long as the nature of little girls is still the same. She wants to be told ahead of time exactly what's right and when. She wants to know exactly how much she loves this person, and exactly what choices this entails. To counter her insistent demand, James repeatedly, in the second half of the novel, holds up to us a different picture: that of an actress who finds, suddenly, that her script is not written in advance and that she must 'quite heroically' improvise her role.... The final understanding to which his criticism of little girls transports us is that *this* is what adult deliberation is and should be. And there's no safety in that, no safety at all.[10]

What conclusions are we meant to draw from these remarks? Surely, that adult deliberation in morals involves imaginative discernment, openness to risk, readiness to venture into uncharted waters, the rejection of safety, and narrowing perspectives. This is certainly how it strikes Diamond. She compares the themes explored by Nussbaum in discussing *The Golden Bowl* with a wider picture associated with James: "In James' novel, *The Europeans*, Gertrude Wentworth is different from the other American characters. The difference is marked at the beginning of the novel by her not going to the church with the others and by her reading *The Arabian Nights* instead. She is reading about the love of Prince Camaralzaman and Princess Badoura when her European cousin, previously unknown to her, turns up. When she looks up and sees this totally unexpected visitor, he is transformed by her imagination into Prince Camaralzaman.... She will not turn away from adven-

9. Ibid., pp. 131, 133.
10. Ibid., p. 138.

ture, nor dry up like a pea in its shell.... The greater danger is *inatten-*
tion, the refusal of adventure."[11]

We can recognize these as elucidations of the examples in question.
We may admire what they show us. But for Nussbaum's philosophical
thesis, more is needed; the examples must present the *sine qua non* of
what adult deliberation is and should be. But they do not amount to
that. Rather, the examples provide the features of a *specific* moral perspective. It is extremely misleading to present the examples, philosophically, in any other light. It is easy to exclude different moral perspectives within which there are very different reactions to similar
situations. Nussbaum might say that the reactions she admires are
adult, whereas the others are childish, but that would be a moral judgment on her part. What she has not shown, and could not show, is that
such a distinction is demanded by philosophical reflection—but that is
her claim. Ironically, the depiction of an openness of the moral imagination in James as the sine qua non of moral reflection *is itself a lack of
philosophical openness* in its failure to recognize different moral possibilities. A specific moral point of view is being presented as though it captured, philosophically, what the parameters of our concern with values
must be.

The moral differences not covered by the examples provided can
be brought out by comparing Diamond's remarks on *The Europeans,*
which I will consider, with a novel by James's underrated contemporary
Edith Wharton. In *The Age of Innocence* a visitor arrives from Europe,
Countess Olenska, to disturb the cozy social hierarchy of upper-
middle-class New York. Newland Archer, already betrothed, is chosen
to persuade the countess not to divorce her husband and so avoid
bringing scandal on an established family. In the course of making his
case, Archer and Countess Olenska fall in love with each other. She is
seen by him as offering escape from everything that is narrow and re-
stricting in his society: the pseudo respectability and stifling social pro-
tocol. In short, she offers adventure of a kind to which Nussbaum gives
such a central place. Archer is all for embarking on it, but he has put
the case for family honor all too well. He succeeds in getting Countess
Olenska to see possibilities of serious sacrifice in what for him had
been merely a nominal code. Her moral imagination transforms his
own view of life. Ellen Olenska says to him: "New York simply meant

11. Cora Diamond, "Missing the Adventure," in *The Realistic Spirit,* p. 315.

peace and freedom to me: it was coming home.... I felt that there was
no one as kind as you; no one who gave me reasons that I understand
for doing what at first seemed so hard and—unnecessary. The very
good people didn't convince me; I felt they'd never been tempted. But
you knew; you understood; you had felt the world outside tugging at
one with all its golden hands—and yet you hated the things it asks of
one; you hated happiness brought by disloyalty and cruelty and indif-
ference. That was what I'd never known before—and it's better than
anything I've known." Archer appeals to rights, their right to happiness. Olenska replies, "Ah, you've taught me what an ugly word that
is."[12] They part, never to meet again.

Here is a morality that chooses to miss the adventure to which Nussbaum invites us. If seriousness is equated with accepting the invitation
and turning away from adventure is equated with drying up like a pea
in a shell, one will be unable to appreciate the possibilities of seriousness Edith Wharton endeavors to show us. All one will see is waste. Indeed, that is all many critics did see.[13] Their responses can be summed
up in the words of Edmund Wilson, who notes that Countess Olenska
"returns to the United States to intrude upon and disturb the existence
of a conservative provincial society.... [S]he attracts and almost capti-
vates an intelligent man of the community who turns out, in the long
run, to be unable to muster the courage to take her, and who allows
her to go back to Europe."[14] For Wilson, Wharton was depicting a
morality of inertia, and Archer was a man to whom nothing was ever
going to happen; what we are shown is a couple who come to a mo-
mentous decision. The value it has is not a function of adventure but of
an adventure being refused in the name of an age-old value of personal
sacrifice.

My aim, of course, is not to argue, in the name of philosophy, for either Nussbaum's emphasis or what Wharton shows us. If a discussion
between them were to ensue, no matter how 'open' it might be, one
cannot determine, philosophically, the direction in which it *ought* to

---

12. Edith Wharton, *The Age of Innocence* (London: Lehmann, 1953), pp. 139–40, 141.
   13. For a fuller discussion of these critics and Wharton's novel, see my "Allegiance
and Change in Morality: A Study in Contrasts," in *Through a Darkening Glass* (Notre
Dame: University of Notre Dame Press; Oxford: Blackwell, 1982).
   14. Edmund Wilson, "Justice to Edith Wharton," in *Edith Wharton: A Collection of Critical Essays,* ed. Irving Howe (Englewood Cliffs, N.J.: Prentice-Hall, 1962), p. 26.

go. Morally, it could go either way, or the disputants might reach no agreement. What is important, philosophically, is to recognize these possibilities and how they throw light on what moral differences are like and the diverse ways in which they enter our lives.

An *absolute* distinction between 'the expansive' and 'the narrow', 'the mature' and 'the immature', 'the adult' and 'the childish' cannot be drawn in such a way that it can be used to discriminate between moralities. Of course, one moral perspective may criticize another in these terms, but then these are moral judgments, not philosophical attempts to transcend them. For example, consider again James's distinction in *The Europeans* between the narrowness of those who go to church and the expansiveness of those who give themselves up to adventure. Diamond says that the danger of the New England spirit for James is that one misses out on life. No doubt one does 'miss out' on much if one is a Puritan. Every morality has a price. Morally, the question concerns what one is prepared to pay. But one also 'misses out' by not being a Puritan—perhaps a simplicity of spirit that may have something to say about the endless analyses in some of James's novels. What cannot be justified philosophically is to call the Puritan spirit 'a denial of life', as though 'denial of life' is a neutral means by which we can determine what is to count as adult moral reflection. If we are making a moral judgment about a Puritan morality, all well and good, but it is philosophically important to recognize that that morality, too, has had something to say about what it takes to be the way, the truth, and the life—about what it is to possess life more abundantly.

Nussbaum, it seems to me, would have difficulty in finding *logical* space for religious moralities. Yet, if we turn to a writer such as Flannery O'Connor and give her the kind of attention Nussbaum gives to Henry James, it would be difficult to argue that religious responses necessarily deaden the detail of human life. To appreciate this, however, one would have to give up an assumption, shared by such writers as Nussbaum and Bernard Williams, that religion is an attempt to deny or make oneself immune from chance and contingency in human life.[15] In fact, concept formation in belief in the gods or in God is internally related to the recognition of those very features of our existence. Nussbaum would have to pay attention to O'Connor's insistence

---

15. See, for example, Bernard Williams's treatment of the gods and contingency in *Shame and Necessity* (Berkeley: University of California Press, 1993). For my criticism [of

that if a writer wants to make the supernatural believable, maximum justice must be done to the natural.

What O'Connor does to the features of human life that Nussbaum thinks important is, of course, very different from what she empha- sizes. But because these features too are part of the sense people find in life, it deserves a philosopher's attention. We see that human life can be like *that*. For example, consider the desire for safety and the denial of contingency in life. In Flannery O'Connor's "The Artificial Nigger," Mr. Head thinks he is perfectly safe; he knows it all. On a journey to the city from the countryside, he is going to demonstrate his self- sufficiency to his young grandson, Nelson. To teach Nelson how de- pendent he is on his grandfather, Mr. Head hides from his grandson when he falls asleep in the city. He thinks the young boy will cry out for him when he wakes and that he will then go to the aid of the lost one. What actually happens is that the young boy panics and runs away. His grandfather cannot keep up with him. In his hurry, the boy sends a woman sprawling, upsetting her groceries and injuring her ankle. By the time the old man arrives, the angry woman is threatening to call the police. The young boy runs to his grandfather, clutching his hand, but the old man denies all knowledge of him, to the horror of the crowd that has gathered. Mr. Head and Nelson stumble off into the darkness. The old man cannot find his way back to the station and calls out in desperation for directions from passersby. He confesses to every- one that he is lost. The visit to the city has shaken both the boy and his grandfather out of their self-sufficiency. Mr. Head has always deni- grated black people, but on the way to the station, he and Nelson are drawn together before a plaster statue of a black man, the kind called an "artificial nigger." The mouth of the statue was chipped so that it was impossible to say whether the person was supposed to be young or old, happy or unhappy: "The two of them stood there with their necks forward at almost the same angle and their shoulders curved in almost exactly the same way and their hands trembling identically in their pockets. Mr. Head looked like an ancient child and Nelson like a miniature old man. They stood gazing at the artificial Negro as if they were faced with some great mystery, some monument to another's vic- tory that brought them together in their common defeat. They could

---

Williams], see "Suspended from Heaven: Ethics, Religion, and Modernity," *Archivio Di Filosofia* (1996).

both feel it dissolving their differences like an action of mercy. Mr. Head had never known before what mercy felt like because he had been too good to deserve any, but he felt he knew now."[16]

Nussbaum also emphasizes the role of 'the surprising' in human life and how it may upset our surest intentions and promises. But what could be more surprising than the act of the grandmother in O'Connor's story "A Good Man Is Hard to Find"? As a result of a car breakdown on a holiday, she encounters the Misfit, who has escaped from the penitentiary. His gang takes her son and his wife and children into the woods, where they are shot. Suddenly, the grandmother, who up to this point has been depicted as an annoying, silly old woman, reaches out and touches the Misfit, saying, "Why, you're one of my babies." She too is shot by the Misfit, but not before he has sprung back from this totally unexpected act of grace.[17]

I have been saying that philosophical contemplation needs to take account of religious perspectives, having criticized critics who fail to recognize them. But, equally, philosophical contemplation needs to take account of secular perspectives, which some critics also fail to recognize. In the course of writing *From Fantasy to Faith,* I encountered Christian critics who wanted to appropriate Hemingway's Old Man, fighting with the giant marlin, and Nathanael West's Miss Lonelyhearts, fighting against religious sentimentality in the face of suffering, as Christ figures. They failed to acknowledge nonreligious moralities.

The differences from which we can learn in philosophical contemplation are many. Coleridge's Ancient Mariner was able to bless the slimy snakes that came out of the sea, whereas Hemingway's Old Man could never have blessed the scavenger sharks that reduced the dead marlin to a skeleton—they lacked style. When we think of moral development, we are probably not thinking of Isaac Babel's initiation as a Red Cossock warrior. On the other hand, when we read Barbara Pym or Flannery O'Connor, the religious beliefs they write of cannot be dismissed as the fantasies of Frank Baum's *Wizard of Oz* or the denials of the human exposed in the poetry of Wallace Stevens.[18]

16. Flannery O'Connor, "The Artificial Nigger," in *The Complete Stories* (New York: Farrar, Straus and Giroux, 1981).

17. See Flannery O'Connor, "A Good Man Is Hard to Find," in *The Complete Stories,* p. 132.

18. For essays on these authors, see Phillips, *From Fantasy to Faith.*

I have stressed that the *kind* of understanding of these possibilities
that philosophical contemplation brings comes from wrestling with
seeing what sort of role moral and religious possibilities play in human
life. Recognizing their heterogeneity plays an important part in this
task. If, on the other hand, we say, like Nussbaum, that moral philosophy benefits from the style of 'telling' that we find in literature, benefits in such a way as to aid us in the task of living well, we are confronted
by questions: Which 'telling' do we have in mind, and in which direction is the guidance supposed to lie?[19] Literature shows as great a variety as life itself. What the differences show is how life can be, but recognizing them cannot be equated with personal appropriation.

What I have called a contemplative conception of philosophy can
be elucidated further by comparing Nussbaum's appeal to literature
with earlier appeals to literature from a Wittgensteinian tradition in
ethics. Both appeals are partly in protest against what moral philosophy makes of morality. For example, as Philippa Foot showed in her
early paper "When Is a Principle a Moral Principle?" it will not do to
argue, as C. L. Stevenson did in *Ethics and Language,* that there is an external relation between commendation and its object. Just as we cannot feel afraid or proud of *anything,* so we cannot call anything we like
good or evil. For this reason, moral principles cannot be characterized
in purely formal terms. As Foot points out, the principle "Never wear
brightly colored clothes" can fulfill all the requirements of R. M. Hare's
universalizability requirement in *The Language of Morals,* as can the rule
"Always wear a hat on Wednesdays." Yet, as Foot shows, unless we are
told more, we cannot see how these are moral principles. A background in which certain concepts are at work is necessary if we are to
appreciate a principle as a moral principle. For instance, if "Never wear
brightly colored clothes" is a rule of a Puritan community, we can see
how its connection with ostentation can give it moral sense. But think
of how different the significance of ostentation is in the societies of
which Henry James and Edith Wharton wrote. Foot points out the importance that a range of concepts such as 'honesty', 'sincerity', 'murder', 'stealing', 'ostentation', and 'treachery' have "in making it possible for us to grasp another man's views on matters of right and wrong,

19. I am putting aside the large question of the difference between learning from a
novel and learning from life. Simone Weil observed that in literature, the portrayal of
evil is interesting, whereas the attempt to portray goodness tends to be boring; in life,
the reverse is true. There, evil is boring, and goodness is interesting.

and it would be interesting to ask how far we could get on without them."[20]

Foot does not say that *all* these concepts must be present in a person's morality or that they must be given the same weight by every person. What she insists on, rightly, is that without such concepts we should have difficulty in understanding where a person stands morally and that the connections made may surprise us. Foot says: "Concepts of this kind enable a man to connect new, and possibly surprising, applications of 'good' or 'bad' with one particular set of other cases—to say, e.g., that wearing bright colours is bad in the same way as boasting."[21]

Foot's point allows for a variety of moral views. Given that people do have such views, Foot emphasizes that it does not follow from her arguments that everyone must *discuss* matters of right and wrong in the same way. But in her later essays "Moral Beliefs" and "Moral Arguments," included in her collection *Virtues and Vices,* the moral variety allowed in the earlier essay disappears. Foot now seeks to give the moral concepts she involves a point, a rationale. That point is first expressed in terms of the self-interest of any individual, strong or weak, and later expressed in terms of the common good. At its most extreme, the later argument led to the view that moral disagreement is some kind of aberration that occurs only because the facts are underdescribed. The earlier essays can accommodate a contemplative conception of philosophy, whereas the later essays cannot.[22]

Moral considerations are not the means of realizing self-interest or something called 'the common good'. Rather, they are constitutive of our readings of situations, what we take the situations and the alternatives facing us to be. A person's moral character, or lack of it, will show itself in what he or she thinks is or is not open to him or her. Nussbaum speaks as though character were an end of our actions. It is something that shows *in* our actions. Thus, despite the many popular offers to build character, as though it were an end for which a therapeutic means can be found, the unrecognized feature of such offers is precisely their lack of character. One does not develop a moral character by thinking of one's deeds as the means of attaining it. If one is honest

---

20. Philippa Foot, "When Is a Principle a Moral Principle?" *Proceedings of the Aristotelian Society,* Supplementary vol. (1954): 108.

21. Ibid.

22. Ibid., p. 109. For more detailed criticisms of Philippa Foot's views, see D. Z. Phillips, *Interventions in Ethics* (London: Macmillan, 1992).

because one wants to have an honest character, one will find oneself thinking about oneself, the image of oneself.

These points can be emphasized by looking at Winch's discussion of Tolstoy's *Father Sergius*. Sergius abandoned a brilliant military career to become a monk, but intertwined with his genuine religious feeling is a desire for preeminence. He becomes famous for his saintliness. Crowds visit him, and people bring their sick to be healed by him. In the middle part of his career, a society woman visits him and attempts to seduce him. Attracted by her though he is, he resists. But, later in his career, he is seduced by a young girl who is retarded and has been sent to him for healing: "'What is your name?' he asked, trembling all over and feeling that he was overcome and that his desire had already passed beyond control. 'Marie. Why?' She took his hand and kissed it, and then put her arm around his waist and pressed him to herself. 'What are you doing?' he said. 'Marie, you are a devil!' 'Oh perhaps. What does it matter?' And embracing him she sat down with him on the bed."[23]

Winch concentrates on the question, "What does it matter?" Sergius was able to resist the earlier attempt at seduction because he could meet it from within the perspective of a genuine religious belief, tempted though he was. As Winch puts it:

> It was not then a case of setting the satisfaction of his desire alongside the demands of his religion and choosing between them. The fulfilment of his religious duties was not then for him an object to be achieved. But this is what it *had* become for him at the time he succumbed to temptation and this indeed is precisely why he succumbed. Marie's question 'What does it matter?' invited a judgement explaining why religious purity is more important than the satisfaction of lust, a comparison, as it were, between two different objects. And no such judgement was possible. I do not mean that earlier, at the time of his strength, Sergius *could* have answered the question; the point is that, from that earlier perspective, the question did not arise for him.[24]

In understanding how Sergius's religious perspective determined his reading of the earlier attempt at seduction and how that perspective later broke up, we can also see that, although philosophy is con-

23. Leo Tolstoy, "Father Sergius," in *"The Kreutzer Sonata" and Other Tales* (London: World Classics, 1960), p. 307.

24. Peter Winch, "Moral Integrity," in *Ethics and Action* (London: Routledge, 1972), p. 189.

cerned with the distinction between corrupt and noncorrupt thinking, it cannot itself determine which moral perspective should be embraced. This would itself be to treat such perspectives as external objects of comparison. Winch shows this excellently at the end of his essay in discussing Sergius's reflections shortly before his seduction, after he has had a discussion with a skeptical young professor:

> "Can I have fallen so low?" he thought. "Lord help me! Restore me, my Lord and God!" And he clasped his hands and began to pray.
> The nightingales burst into song, a cockchafer knocked against him and crept up the back of his neck. He brushed it off. "But does He exist? What if I am knocking at a door fastened from outside? The bar is on the door for all to see. Nature—the nightingales and the cockchafers—is that bar. Perhaps the young man was right."[25]

In a letter to an aunt, Tolstoy had written from a perspective very different from that of Father Sergius: "For me, religion comes from life, not life from religion. You scoff at my nature and nightingales. But in my religion, nature is the intermediary."[26] Commenting on this contrast, Winch says that it would be confused to think that one could have a demonstration, independently of the two perspectives, to decide whether nature is a bar or an intermediary. How it will be seen will depend on the perspective of the agent. Moral philosophy cannot be an arbiter in the dispute, no matter how much it reflects on literature. As Winch says: "Neither it, nor any other form of enquiry, can show what *is* worthy of admiration. The idea that it can is itself a form of corruption and always involves an obscuring of possibilities.... Philosophy may indeed try to remove intellectual obstacles in the way of recognizing certain possibilities (though there is always the danger that it will throw up new obstacles). But what a man makes of the possibilities he can comprehend is a matter of what man he is. This is revealed in the way he lives; it is revealed *to him* in his understanding of what he can and what he cannot attach importance to." It is a matter of a person's character, one might say. Winch concludes, rightly, that "philosophy can no more show a man what he should attach importance to than geometry can show a man where he should stand."[27]

This conclusion differs strikingly from the far-reaching ambitions Nussbaum has for literature as moral philosophy. As we have seen, she

25. Tolstoy, "Father Sergius," p. 342.
26. Henri Troyat, *Tolstoy*, trans. Nancy Amphoux (London: W. H. Allen, 1968), p. 186.
27. Winch, "Moral Integrity," p. 191.

hopes that literature will itself bring us to a substantive conception of
what adult deliberation on moral matters amounts to. Such matters as
literature reveals have, she claims, a universal significance. But how can
that be maintained given the particular and diverse moral perspectives
depicted in literature? Her reply is that the novelist shows us something that may actually happen. When a reader appreciates what is
shown, this is something that may happen in his or her life. I do not
think this follows. One's appreciation of a specific moral perspective in
literature may lead one to conclude that one could never see things in
that way.

Nussbaum does not want to say that universal rules can be depicted
in an abstract way from literature, but she does claim of a depiction,
say, of a relationship between father and daughter, "that two people
who had a situation with all the same contextual features, in all of their
historical specificity, ought to act, in many cases at least, in the same
way." But what does saying this amount to? Nussbaum admits that because of the particularity of relationships where love is concerned, it
makes little sense to speak of a universal rule, as though the people involved were replaceable by others as instances of that rule. She wants to
say that even when universality is present, it is not the universality of a
principle to which people have to adhere but of "a direction of thought
and imagination."[28] Again, this observation gives the appearance of
great flexibility, and so it does, as long as one realizes that it is a flexibility *within* the general perspective Nussbaum advocates morally, the
kind one can find in the novels of Henry James. The general difficulty
can be stated by substituting Nussbaum's name for that of Cavell in the
comments by Stephen Mulhall that I noted in Chapter 5: "Anyone who
understands the acknowledgement structure underlying [Nussbaum's]
model of reading would expect [her] to search for and to use texts
which participate in [her] own attitude and approach to reading for
according to the terms of that approach, only texts written in the spirit
in which [she] reads would be capable of calling forth heightened or
exemplary experiences of reading—only texts motivated by the thoughts
and feelings that are crystallized in [Nussbaum's] own conception and
practice of reading[29] could provide words capable of testing and draw-

---

28. Martha Nussbaum, "'Finely Aware and Richly Responsible': Literature and the
Moral Imagination," in *Love's Knowledge*, p. 167.

29. This does not preclude this conception's having been inspired, initially, by works
of literature.

ing out the full potential of that practice."[30] I ask the same question of
Nussbaum as I asked of Cavell: If the examples are chosen because they
are known to be the kind that exemplify human relations (Nussbaum)
wants to advance, they may well draw out the potential in such relations, but in what sense do the examples test them? This question is especially important given the claim that the *kind* of examples show us
the parameters of moral sensitivity. By contrast, a contemplative conception of philosophy demands that we give attention to perspectives
that are *not* ours, an attention we may be reluctant to give them. Such
attention helps us to understand better the different ways the notion of
moral sensitivity is used in human life.

Nussbaum wants to avoid any suggestion of moral relativism. She is
attracted by John Rawls's notion of 'reflective equilibrium', which involves working through "the major alternative views about the good
life, holding them up, in each case, against our own experience and
our intuitions. The first step will be to get a perspicuous description of
these alternatives (though we should bear in mind that these descriptions will already contain an element of evaluation and response)....
Next we notice and clearly describe the tensions and conflicts among
the views that we find. Where there is inconsistency or irreconcilable
tension—and where this tension corresponds to something that we notice in our own thought (individually or communally)—we aim to re-
vise the overall picture so as to bring it into harmony with itself, pre-
serving, as Aristotle says, 'the greatest number and the most basic' of
the original judgements and perceptions."[31]

In the light of Winch's discussion of "Father Sergius," we should be
able to appreciate the artificiality of the proposed program. From
where is 'the working through' the various 'alternatives' to be done?
What is to inform it? An Archimedean point is sought where none exists. A student once wrote an essay for me in which he said that Ivan
Ilych, on his deathbed, decided to change his lifestyle. This comic account of fundamental moral change is one we need to appreciate
philosophically. As we have seen, what is to be regarded as 'an alternative' is itself determined by one's moral perspective. Of course, contact
with other perspectives may change one's own, but the directions of

---

30. See p. 109.
31. Martha Nussbaum, "Perceptive Equilibrium: Literary Theory and Moral Theory,"
in *Love's Knowledge*, pp. 173–74.

change will be as various as the original perspectives. Although they are tensions *within* the experience of an individual, Nussbaum treats the different perspectives as though they are inconsistent views a person tries to hold at the same time. When the different perspectives are seen as the *different* views of individuals or groups, they are not 'incomplete' and awaiting a more comprehensive harmonization. And if 'living in harmony' is prized, even though the peace is kept, it does not follow that it is the highest value. As seen in my discussion of Rorty, it may simply be the necessary condition, at a given time, of pursuing what *is* valued most, without interference.

Nussbaum is at great pains to show how what may seem to be widely different outlooks nevertheless contribute to the 'reflective equilibrium'. In Henry James's *The Ambassadors,* it may first appear that a wide disparity exists between the safe moral outlook of Mrs. Newsome and Strether's sense of adventure and moral risk. But this is not so. The sense of risk and adventure can lead to a revision of the notion of 're-flective equilibrium' by getting us to realize that

> emotions may after all in many cases be an invaluable guide to correct judgement; that general and universal formulations may be inadequate to the complexity of particular situations; that immersed particular judgements may have a value that reflective and general judgements cannot capture. We want to suggest that bewilderment and hesitation may actually be marks of fine attention.... There is still a search for equilibrium here, as Strether tries to make it all "hang beautifully together".... But his equilibrium, dealing, as it does, with impressions, emotions, and, in general, with particulars, had better be called by a different name. We would do better, perhaps, to call it "perceptive equilibrium": an equilibrium in which concrete perceptions "hang beautifully together", both with one another and with the agent's general principles; an equilibrium that is always ready to reconstitute itself in response to the new.[32]

It will be clear from these remarks that even though 'reflective equilibrium' has been modified to being a 'perceptive equilibrium', the aim of harmony has not changed. Nussbaum admits that the reflective processes she advocates involve value judgments, but because she has argued that such judgments constitute the openness of moral imagination and sensitivity, she is not deterred from her 'holistic enterprise'. Nussbaum writes that these "procedures themselves are value-laden,

32. Ibid., p. 182.

and thus part and parcel of the holistic enterprise they organize; replaceable, like any other part, to the end of deeper and more inclusive attunement. So we must examine them at each stage, asking whether they are capable of doing full justice to everything that our sense of life wants to include."[33]

We have already seen that what we regard as "replaceable" will itself be determined by one's moral perspective. Moreover, as we have seen earlier in this chapter and in our discussions of Cavell and Rorty, "deeper and more inclusive attunement" is not a context-free regulative idea transcending all moralities but is itself a value that some will pursue enthusiastically, others accept reluctantly, and yet others not want at all. Further, the appeal to "our sense of life" invokes an unearned universality, all the more difficult to realize because of the language of openness and flexibility employed. By contrast, the universality to which a contemplative conception of philosophy draws our attention is one that demands perspicuous representations of moral distances, temporary and permanent, as well as of moral proximities and compromises. This universality, unlike the one Nussbaum talks of, is *not* a moral ideal. It is the product of a philosophical attention that says, Human life can be like that. Nussbaum's notion of universality attempts to rescue the principle of universalizability from inadequacies she recognizes, but an appeal to literature should show her that these inadequacies are far more extensive than she realizes.

In discussing Melville's *Billy Budd, Foretopman,* Winch shows that Captain Vere is faced with a moral dilemma in deciding the fate of Billy Budd, a person of angelic character who has killed the satanic master-at-arms, Claggart, who had been tormenting him. Faced with the false accusation of inciting the crew to mutiny, Billy cannot defend himself because, with the stress, his speech impediment reduces him to stammering. He strikes Claggart, who falls and dies as a result of striking his head. The choice facing Vere is not between morality and military law but between what are, for him, conflicting moral obligations. On the one hand, there is the question of whether he can condemn to death a man innocent before God. On the other hand, there is the imperial conscience of the military code. It is important to remember that even after having condemned Billy to death, Vere still feels the full force of the fact that he has condemned a man innocent before God. If we take that away we miss the tragedy in the story.

33. Ibid., p. 186.

Winch says that he could not have come to Vere's decision: "In reaching this decision I do not think that I should appeal to any considerations over and above those to which Vere himself appeals. It is just that I think I should find the considerations connected with Billy Budd's peculiar innocence too powerful to be overridden by an appeal to military duty."[34] Nevertheless, Winch does not feel committed to saying, as the principle of universalizability insists that he should, that what Vere did was wrong. The issue between Winch and those who disagree with him is not whether they agree with his moral judgment that Vere did what was right for him but whether they will allow his reaction to be a moral judgment at all. Winch is not denying that someone may say that what Vere did was wrong. He has no philosophical objection to this. What he objects to is a view that has no logical space for his view.

Nussbaum would fear, no doubt, that Winch's phrase 'right for him' introduces the moral relativism she wants to avoid. Does it not lead to that Protagorean relativism which says that what is right is whatever an individual says is right? Winch shows how Vere's relation to his decision, the character of his reflectiveness, will not allow this to be said of him. He also shows, to repeat what I said in the last chapter, that there are checks that would stop us, in certain circumstances, from being able to say, "He did what was right for him." A person may show no concern with moral considerations, or the concern that he or she does show may be riddled by self-deception. Winch also recognizes that there will be moral or psychological barriers in different people that may well prevent them from calling certain perspectives moral. Yet too great a restriction on what one can recognize may get in the way of philosophy's contemplative task.

If we want to express how the situation strikes the person confronting Vere's dilemma, "we cannot dispense with his inclination to come to a particular moral decision. Thus the situation at the court-martial struck Vere very differently from the way it struck the senior officer of marines, who was for acquitting Billy. But what did this difference consist in? Surely in the fact that, faced with two conflicting sets of considerations, the one man was disposed to give precedence to the one and acquit, and the other, to give precedence to the other and convict."[35] Philosophical contemplation shows how, by giving attention

34. Peter Winch, "The Universalizability of Moral Judgements," in *Ethics and Action*, p. 163.
35. Ibid., p. 169.

to both responses, we appreciate that these are final reasons for the people concerned. It is a corruption of this inquiry to ascribe to it the task, through reflection, of seeking a harmony between these responses. If this is true of situations involving court-martials, how much more is it likely to be true of the sphere of personal relationships?

Because of the holistic character of her moral enterprise, Nussbaum finds it impossible to apply it to sexual love between human beings, which leads to her remarkable exclusion of this love from the sphere of morality. When one brings sexual love and morality together, she claims, "the goal might not be equilibrium at all, but a dynamic tension between two possible irreconcilable visions." Nussbaum claims that we become aware "of the deep elements in our emotional life that in their violence or intensity lead us outside of the ethical attitude altogether."[36] Elaborating on what this comes to she says: "For so long as our eyes are open, we are wonderful and lovable and finely responsive; but when we immerse ourselves in the most powerful responses, entering silence, closing our eyes, are we then capable at all of asking questions about our friends, of thinking of the good of the community?"[37] If *that* is what the ethical must be to be involved in love, it is little wonder that Nussbaum sees morality and love as mutually exclusive. But what is depicted is nearer to comic misunderstanding then to dynamic tension.

When we turn from such examples to Newland Archer's and Ellen Olenska's decision not to elope in *The Age of Innocence,* we see that their choice is unintelligible without taking into account the interpenetration of love and the ethical. It is this interpenetration which shows why Anna Karenina's passion cannot sustain her relationship with Vronsky over time. She wants love to be an "eternal beginning," unmediated and therefore not addressing the details of their relationship and situation.[38]

Consider a very different kind of love and the depth it portrays. I am thinking of Mario's silent, secret love in Thomas Mann's *Mario and the Magician* and what is involved in his being made to reveal it under hypnosis before a derisive audience. Rush Rhees analyzes the degradation involved:

36. Nussbaum, "Perceptive Equilibrium," p. 190.

37. Ibid., p. 189.

38. See D. Z. Phillips, "Ethics and Anna Karenina," in *Literature and Ethics,* proceedings from a symposium, Norwegian Academy of Science and Letters, Oslo, 1992.

The most obvious is: (1) that there's something terrible about being tricked into surrendering *this* secret, which there would not be with a secret of any other sort. The second is: (2) that what is degrading and destructive of Mario is that he is brought by the hypnotist to make the exposure *himself*—in fact, no one else *could* have exposed Mario's innermost feelings and so degrade them.

About (1): Suppose a man did something ugly and disgraceful in the past, and he's terrified now lest it come to light. He was responsible for the downfall of his friend, when his friend thought all along that he was loyal; or perhaps he took part in some widely known and disgraceful crime. Suppose I discover and expose this. He may be broken and kill himself. Then I've done something foul, I think. But I should not have brought about the degradation of the man in the way that Cipolla, the hypnotist, did with Mario. What Mario exposes of himself is *not* disgraceful. If it had been, it would not have been "what was innermost in him", in the sense in which Mann is speaking. If Cipolla had revealed something disgraceful about Mario's past—then Mario might have grown red faced and hung his head and returned to his place or left the hall. As it was, Mario could not do that.

This is one point: what is degrading and destructive here is not the exposure of anything *evil* or shameful, nothing to make him feel overwhelmed by guilt or disgrace.

Another is (2): Suppose that nothing had happened except that Mario's companion, Giovanotto, told the audience of Mario's love for Sylvestra and laughed about it. Then Mario might have grown bitter and felt sickened, but he could have kept his dignity. There would have been no degradation of *him,* even if one felt that Giovanotto had sunk pretty low. What makes the difference is that Mario *himself* is brought to expose the madly ecstatic devotion that is innermost in him.... Nothing that anyone else could have 'discovered' and told about Mario's love would ever have been—or been anything like—what Mario himself showed.[39]

I have quoted Rhees's analysis at some length to show one instance of the interpenetration of love and the ethical. Just try understanding Rhees's analysis without it.

Two more examples: Wittgenstein discussed with Rhees the predicament of a man who has to choose between giving up his cancer research and leaving his wife. It may seem as though anyone else could

---

39. Rush Rhees, "The Tree of Nebuchadnezzar," in Rhees, *Moral Questions,* ed. D. Z. Phillips (London: Macmillan, 1999). Originally published in two parts in the *Human World,* no. 4 (August 1971) and no. 6 (February 1972).

continue his research and that the choice is obvious. But he may know that if he gives up his work he will go to pieces and drag her down with him. Here, Wittgenstein says, "we have all the materials of a tragedy.... Whatever he finally does, the way things then turn out may affect his attitude. He may say, 'Well, thank God I left her; it was better all round.' Or maybe, 'Thank God I stuck to her.' Or he may not be able to say 'thank God' at all, but just the opposite. I want to say that this is the solution of an ethical problem."[40]

Nussbaum's neglect of the interpenetration of love and the ethical comes from her holistic characterization of the latter. And yet it is obvious that some of the most difficult problems human beings face come from this aspect of their lives. Rhees is surprised by the neglect of this fact in the work of Simone Weil and, he thinks, in Christianity more generally. He admired Simone Weil's discussion of suffering and its "freedom from every shade of self-assertion or consideration of effect—what she herself calls the 'nakedness' of the style she strove for."

> [Yet] the situation of a man and woman whose marriage is breaking up, she *never* considers, so far as I know. I am thinking especially of the case where it is breaking up although they love one another (it would not be so terrible otherwise), and although the break is not the result of any clear wrong done by either partner. Eugene O'Neill wrote about situations near to this in some of his plays. "If only they had loved one another enough ..." Good Christ, if only they *hadn't* loved one another.... the relation of man and woman. The relation of parent and child. Relations without which there would be no life. Relations in which the love goes deep—and breaks people. I do not think these are ever considered in religion. Christ never considers them. The love of one's neighbour, of which he speaks, is the love of a stranger in distress, who will never be seen again.
>
> Strange, in one way. Because the tragedy which comes from the love of parents and children is so much a theme of Jewish stories.[41]

I have contrasted Nussbaum's appeal to literature with earlier and recent appeals to literature from within a Wittgensteinian tradition in ethics. That tradition has not been well received in ethics because its

---

40. Rhees, "Some Developments in Wittgenstein's View of Ethics," in *Discussions of Wittgenstein* (London: Routledge, 1970), pp. 99–100.

41. Rush Rhees, from a letter to M. O'C. Drury, 24 May 1962, Rush Rhees Archive, Department of Philosophy, University of Wales, Swansea.

contemplative character is not appreciated. As we saw in Chapter 6, Onora O'Neill, one of the few to respond to the tradition at all, criticizes it for not arbitrating between the excellent examples it discussed. She does not appreciate that the examples provided were not 'incomplete', awaiting further moral discussions. They were meant to be examples of people *already* making decisions in very different ways—examples that would show the ways such decisions enter human life. What is more, their use in moral philosophy constituted a break within the same features of Anglo-Saxon moral philosophy against which Nussbaum protests. As Peter Winch said:

> In moral as in other branches of philosophy good examples are indispensable: examples, that is, which bring out the real force of the ways in which we speak and in which language is not 'on holiday' (to adapt a remark of Wittgenstein's). It is needful to say this in opposition to a fairly well-established, but no less debilitating, tradition in recent Anglo-Saxon moral philosophy, according to which it is not merely possible, but desirable, to take *trivial* examples. The rationale of this view is that such examples do not generate the emotion which is liable to surround more serious cases and thus enable us to look more coolly at the logical issues involved. On such a view what is characteristic of the ways in which we express our moral concerns can be examined quite apart from any consideration of what it is about those concerns which makes them important to us. But "a moral use that does not matter" is a mere chimera.[42]

But in 1970, C. W. K. Mundle reacted to the Wittgensteinian tradition as we have seen Onora O'Neill do later, saying that there was "a method of teaching ethics [which] has become popular in parts of Wales and England. This is to read long extracts from Russian novels or Existentialist plays, describing dilemmas.... [W]hen well done, this is an excellent way of starting arguments about what you would have done in the problem situations. And, sometimes, about why."[43]

In both reactions, we see a resistance to a contemplative conception of philosophy. In the appeal to literature, what is shown is not the attainment of understanding but the portrayal of it.[44] Nussbaum moves from this portrayal to its personal appropriation. For her, the portray-

---

42. Winch, "The Universalizability of Moral Judgements," p. 155.

43. C. W. K. Mundle, *A Critique of Linguistic Philosophy* (Oxford: Clarendon Press, 1970), p. 14.

44. I owe this comment to Rush Rhees.

als are meant to help us to live well. Cora Diamond has doubts about this aspect of her work:

> There may even be a tension between Martha Nussbaum's account of ethics in terms of the good life and James's interests. His description of his aim (the production of an 'intelligent report' of experience, i.e., of 'our apprehension and measure of what happens to us as social creatures') brings him, she says, "into intimate connection with the Aristotelian enterprise".... But is the relation so close? That James and Aristotle can both be described as concerned with the 'appearances', with people's 'experiences and sayings', does not settle the question. James's interest is that of a 'painter'; his 'report of people's experience' is essentially his 'appreciation' of it, and to appreciate is to avoid as far as possible all simplification (simplification which would be in place if one's concern were action and practical application), to convey the sense and taste of a situation through intimacy with a man's specific behaviour, intimacy with his given case, and so to see that case as a whole. He certainly does not explicitly say anything about the good life for human beings, nor even imply that there *is* such a thing. And even if he did believe there is such a thing, an interest in moral features of human life need not (in general) be an interest in what the good human life would be.[45]

The temptation to go beyond a contemplative conception of philosophy is extremely powerful. We have already seen how Foot wanted to go beyond her early essay "When Is a Principle a Moral Principle?" which has Wittgensteinian affinities, in the later essays that deny the heterogeneity of morals. It was interesting, as editor of the series in which Foot's *Virtues and Vices* first appeared, to find her not wanting to include the early essay. We see a similar development in Iris Murdoch. In her early essay, "Vision and Choice in Morality," her emphasis is the same as that of Rhees when he said that morally "the variety is important—not in order to fix your gaze on the unadulterated form, but to keep you from looking for it."[46] Murdoch, too, complains:

> Philosophers have been misled, not only by a rationalistic desire for unity, but also by certain simplified and generalised moral attitudes current in our society, into seeking a single philosophical definition of morality. If, however, we go back again to the data we see that there are fundamentally different moral pictures which different individuals use

---

45. Diamond, "Moral Philosophy," p. 376.
46. Rhees, "Wittgenstein's View of Ethics," p. 102.

or which the same individual uses at different times. Why should philosophy be less various, where the differences in what it attempts to analyse are so important? Wittgenstein says (*Untersuchungen* 226e) that "What has to be accepted, the given, is—so one could say—*forms of life*". For purposes of analysis moral philosophy should remain at the level of the differences, taking the moral forms of life as given, and not try to *get behind them* to a single form.[47]

Yet, when she collected essays in *The Sovereignty of Good* in the series of which I was editor, the earlier essay was not to be included.[48] In the later work, under Simone Weil's influence, she is attracted by the idea of the unity of the virtues and the suggestion that fantasy blinds us to what virtue is. Analysis does not remain at the level of the differences, seeing the places they occupy in our forms of life.

Even when the differences are recognized, one must be careful in expressing the kind of understanding that contemplation of these differences brings us. For example, Raimond Gaita argues that these are differences "from which we may learn, because they are within the space of ... common understanding." But that understanding need not be a common *moral* understanding. We have already seen the difficulty in Cavell's claim that there is a relation of mutual respect between these differences. That may not be the case. In some cases, there will be respect, in others not. Gaita says that 'the sharedness of human life' "enables those differences to speak to us, to have the power to move us, to reveal to us depth where we had not seen it before, and sense where we had not thought it possible." If this does not happen, Gaita argues, "these different perspectives will be mute, because the humanity in them will not be fully present to us."[49]

A lot will depend on what is meant by 'the power to move us', 'to reveal to us depth', and so on. If these terms are meant to be features of personal, moral appropriation, this cannot be so, given that many of the differences recognized are in conflict with one another. Philosophical reflection does not underwrite any specific form of moral appropriation. But neither does it deny that different moral views are critical of one another.[50] This much was clarified in my discussion of Rorty and

47. Murdoch, "Vision and Choice in Morality," p. 57.
48. Iris Murdoch, *The Sovereignty of Good* (London: Routledge, 1970).
49. Raimond Gaita, critical notice of *Interventions in Ethics*, by D. Z. Phillips, *Philosophical Investigations* 17, 4 (October 1994): 625.
50. The fear that it does is found in Robert C. Roberts, "Kierkegaard, Wittgenstein, and a Method of 'Virtue Ethics,'" in *Kierkegaard and Post/Modernity*, ed. Martin J.

Rhees in Chapter 4. But its interest is a different one: the recognition that life can be like that, including its moral distances and proximities. What 'the sharedness of human life' comes to here is not 'the sharedness' of a specific moral perspective but the hubbub of voices in human discourse. This diversity demands an attention to things that we constantly wish to go beyond. In this chapter, I have explored that wish in relation to Nussbaum's use of literature in moral philosophy—the wish connected with her exhilaration at the thought of the task a moral philosopher can perform. By contrast, others have seen that ambition as a corruption of philosophical contemplation. What that contemplation provides in relation to literature is not inspiration for living well but a cool place for characters. It is in this cool place that philosophical understanding of the possibility of discourse resides.

At the end of Chapters 6 and 7, it may seem to many readers that the philosophical neutrality I have sought to rescue from foundational distortions of itself, is itself simply an optional conception of philosophy that I seek to impose on others. But, as I have said, the nature of philosophy is a philosophical issue. I do not deny that use may be made of philosophical distinctions and expertise in the elucidation and advocacy of specific moral perspectives. It is another matter, however, to claim that such perspectives are *underwritten* by philosophy. In criticizing this claim I am not *imposing* a conception of philosophy on anyone but rather arguing, philosophically, for an alternative. My claim has been that foundationalism, though obsolete in some of its older forms, is still with us in forms that, though harder to detect, are just as misleading.

By contrast, I have emphasized a wonder that, I believe, is as old as philosophy itself—wonder at the possibility of discourse, at the fact that people have spoken and still speak to one another in various ways. This is not to set up any kind of transcendental project, any kind of demonstration of the conditions of discourse, conditions that seek to get behind, in some way, the possibilities exemplified *in* discourse itself. It is in contemplating these possibilities in wrestling with philosophical problems that we are engaged in the struggle to go nowhere.

Marustik and Merold Westphal (Bloomington: Indiana University Press, 1995), pp. 159–65.

8

Trying to Go Nowhere:
An Autobiographical Afterword

From the time of my first academic job in Queen's College, Dundee, Scotland, in 1961, then part of the University of St. Andrews, I have always had an interest in teaching continuing education courses in addition to my other teaching duties. That tradition of liberal education is being destroyed in Britain by the insistence that each course, to be funded, must lead to a certificate, diploma, or degree. To receive support, students in continuing education must show that they are going somewhere.

Different kinds of people attended the old extramural courses: marvelous people who had missed out on a formal, advanced education; graduates in one subject who wanted to pursue informal interests in others; and, of course, dilettantes who wanted to tell their friends they were up on the latest thing. In this last group was a woman who asked me every week, "Who's top in philosophy now?" and accepted with evident satisfaction my intended deflationary reply, "Russell's in front by a short head, but Wittgenstein's coming up fast on the outside." She wanted to know who was going somewhere, and now, alas, so does the government.

I need not tell you that these attitudes can be found in academia too. On a visit to Claremont, a deconstructionist asked one of my graduate students what was going on there in theology and the philosophy of religion. He was told of the familiar fluctuation of student interest at Claremont between process theology and analytic philosophy of religion. Asking who was working there in the latter field, he was told "D. Z. Phillips," to which he replied, "He's going nowhere." To be found "not guilty" of this accusation, I would have to convince the deconstructionist that I was going somewhere or, better, that, like him, presumably, I had already got somewhere, in which case, I suppose, I would have to be going somewhere else—on to ever better things. After all, one might ask, isn't that a reasonable goal for any self-respecting worker? Isn't there a job to be done, something to be achieved? Shouldn't I be concerned about the deconstructionist's verdict, even worried by it? Who would want one's graduate students to know, not to mention the Board of Fellows or the College Council, that one was going nowhere?

And yet I have to tell you that for the thirty-eight years I have been teaching philosophy, that is exactly what I have been trying to do—to go nowhere. I say *trying*, because this is one of the most difficult things to do in philosophy—to go nowhere. In this brief afterword, I would like to reiterate why.

Let me begin with an analogy between morality and philosophy that takes us part of the way. In innumerable occupations, there is a commendable emphasis on getting somewhere. The easiest thing is to go nowhere, whereas getting somewhere needs energy and enterprise. Morally, however, the reverse is the case: it is easy to want to be somebody, whether in the street gang or in academia. There is abundant reward and encouragement for doing so: from "who's the toughest guy on the block" to "who's tops in philosophy."

Sometimes there may be disagreements about who has really got somewhere, so it would be extremely useful if there were some common measure to determine this. Obligingly, our society has provided one: money. I recall a minister who was a lecturer in religious studies and who refused to preach unless the fee was right. One day, he called a philosopher friend of mine to the window of the senior common room of the college at which they taught and pointing to a Jaguar in the parking lot said, "Who would ever have thought that teaching religion would lead to my having a car like that. What do you think of it?" My friend replied, "It's a splendid car, but there's only one thing wrong with it." "What's that?" asked the minister anxiously. "Well," said my friend, "you'll have a hell of a time trying to drive it through the eye of a needle!"

I remember my amazement when I first found out that an honorarium was paid for reading papers in American universities, a practice still unheard of in Britain apart from endowed lectures. I recall being near an American town I wanted to see and writing to the department of philosophy at the university there, inquiring whether I could read a paper to them. They said they would like to hear me but were not sure whether they could afford me. In reply I sent a letter saying that an honorarium was unnecessary as long as accommodation could be provided. But I also sent a joke letter, to arrive two days earlier, that listed the papers I had available and the honorarium required for each. This was many years ago, so please remember that prices have risen: "Perception: $50; Proof of an External World: $150," and so on, culminating with "Humility and Dying to the Self: $1,500." But I was also told in all seriousness, in a famous American divinity school, how mistaken I had been on a visit to organize colloquia for nothing: "No one important does anything for nothing." So the familiar aim is to be something, and encouragement is plentiful.

All this is a far cry from a Wittgenstein who gave up his chair at Cambridge to be free of vanity, only to find it waiting, he said, in his own work. It is a far cry from a Simone Weil who strove for a nakedness of style in her writing in which she said what she did without any flourish or striving for effect. Wittgenstein's concern too was about whether his work "hit the nail on the head." Morally, then, the difficulty is to be a "nobody," especially because, ideally, you would not know if you are one. There is the story of the monastic order that, desperate to be known for something, when others were known for their preaching, learning, contemplation, and so on, said, "Well, at least we're tops in humility." Or the story of the Sunday school teacher who rounded off her lesson on the self-righteousness of the Pharisees by saying, "And aren't we glad, children, that you and I are better than those Pharisees?"

Why is there an analogy between morality and philosophy in this context? Because philosophy, more than any subject, in its metaphysical systems was really concerned with 'going somewhere'. Indeed, it was thought to be philosophy's business to decide whether *any* of our beliefs were 'going somewhere', whether they were rational or irrational. It was thought to be philosophy's distinctive task to test whether our beliefs had the required foundations, whether our modes of discourse reflected reality. This was the Enlightenment ideal: all must be brought to the bar of reason to be judged there. So if philosophy of religion or ethics are to get somewhere, they must show us whether there is a God or what constitutes the good life.

I do not pursue these aims in my work and have not pursued them in the present work. In this sense, I am not trying to go anywhere. It is always fun to deconstruct a deconstructionist—especially if it gets the person to see that he or she is already at a place he or she should not have tried to leave. So when the deconstructionist said, "D. Z. Phillips is going nowhere," I really hope he is right. I am trying to go nowhere, to desist from the philosophical task of showing whether there is a God, proving why we should heed moral considerations, or determining the nature of the good life. But I am not trying to desist from tasks which philosophy can fulfil but which, for some reason or another, I am not interested in. No, I think that the very conception of these tasks is confused—and that itself is a philosophical conclusion. So in criticizing endeavors that may spring from philosophy's deepest concerns, I do not say, "You have not got to the place you want to get to, you should try to go somewhere else" but, more radically, "The very conception of 'the somewhere' you wanted to get to is confused. You should try hard to go nowhere."

But now, it may be said, I am trying to legislate against and prohibit something philosophers have always done. I must know, for example, that political philosophers have criticized forms of government in the light of political ideals they espouse. I must know that moral philosophers have criticized certain kinds of moral motivation in the light of moral ideals they espouse. I must know that some philosophers of religion condemn belief in God, advocate certain attitudes they think should be taken toward other religions, and so on. All this goes on; how can I deny it? The answer is that I do not. What I deny is the claim by the philosophers concerned that the value judgments they make (for that is what they are) are themselves underwritten by philosophy. The subject cannot get them to where they think they are going.

How does it come about that philosophers think they can get to these destinations? One reason, as Wittgenstein shows, is that they sublime the logic of our language. They elevate one kind of discourse and make it the paradigm by which other kinds of discourse are to be judged. These paradigms have varied in the history of philosophy. It has been said that nothing, not even "2 + 2 = 4," can be certain unless we can prove the existence of a God who is no deceiver. It has been said that only the propositions of logic and mathematics are certain and that no empirical proposition can be certain. It has been said that only primary qualities really belong to things, whereas secondary qualities do not. It has been said that only factual propositions are objective, whereas all propositions to do with values are subjective, and so on.

The hard work in philosophy is to bring out why philosophers have made these claims—why they have sublimed the logic of our language. They have done so because important features of our discourse have tempted them, as they tempt us, to do so. That is why one learns from engaging with these difficulties. Unless we see what leads us into them, we can never find our way out of them. As Wittgenstein says, "Our aim is to bring words back from their metaphysical to their ordinary use", where by 'ordinary use' he means the natural contexts in which our concepts have their meaning.[1]

The result is that we come to appreciate the rich variety in human discourse: mathematical discourse, scientific discourse, moral discourse, political discourse, religious discourse. But these are not isolated games, 'complete' without reference to others, but features of the common language, the culture, in which they occur. Within these various contexts we learn to distinguish between truth and falsity, the real and the unreal.

One of the deepest confusions in philosophy is to treat different spheres of discourse as though they themselves were hypotheses concerning a reality that is forever beyond them. But these spheres of discourse do not refer to reality either successfully or unsuccessfully. Rather, they determine, in different contexts, what it means to talk of the real and the unreal.

In contemporary epistemology, it is often said that we must take these contexts on trust, because we can never *know* that they refer to reality. In thinking otherwise, the Enlightenment ideal was mistaken. We do not have the resources to *know* that our spheres of discourse refer to reality. We take them on trust, and it is rational to do so in the absence of anything that serves us better. But justification is by faith, not by reason. Once again, the aim is to 'get somewhere', to make contact with reality, but the way to get there is said to be via trust, not knowledge.

There are two major objections to this view. First, it trades on an abstract notion of reality, to which, of necessity, no content can be given. It speaks of 'reality' as that which gives foundation to our ways of acting and thinking, whereas, as I have said, it is in the context of our ways of acting and thinking that we learn to distinguish the real from the unreal. These ways are the element in which we make our judgments.

---

1. Wittgenstein, *Philosophical Investigations,* I: §116.

Second, on this view, it is assumed that everything we have ever thought or done could be mistaken and that reality, 'how things are', could be entirely different from what we have taken it to be. But this supposition does not make sense.

Consider the view that the whole of mathematics could be mistaken. I may make a mistake in my calculations, but that is itself a mathematical discovery. But if I cannot calculate at all, I do not make a mistake. Rather, I am cut off from calculation, from an extremely important way of understanding the world.

Similarly, if we were cut off from our familiar ways of talking about our physical surroundings and human neighborhood, would we say we had made a mistake? Surely not. For example, if someone could convince you now that you are not where you are, reading these words, but are actually at the other end of the world, reading something quite different, you would not say, "I made a rather big mistake today." Think of it actually happening to you. You would be terrified. Your world would be falling apart. If you had made a mistake, you would need correction. But what you would actually need is treatment.

It may be thought that with morality, matters are different. We do not disagree about what we call calculation or about the fact that we live amid physical surroundings and in a human neighborhood. On the other hand, we do have moral disagreements. As we have seen, we cannot take agreement for granted in this context. But we must be careful to compare like with like. We may disagree over whether someone has repaid a debt, in which case there is no disagreement over the conception of repaying a debt. The only disagreement is over whether *this* individual has repaid a debt. But there can be disagreements not simply within moral perspectives but *between* moral perspectives. There can be different conceptions of satisfying a debt, of satisfying honor. These different conceptions are not hypotheses about a more ultimate moral reality. We may be misled into thinking so, because one moral perspective may call another mistaken or false. But these terms are value judgments, and if they are spelled out, it is in terms of values. As Rush Rhees said, the variety of moral perspectives is important not to fix our gaze on the unadulterated form but to keep us from searching for it. The same conclusions follow when people speak of true and false gods.

Yet it may be thought that an essential difference exists in philosophical discussions of religion. For the most part, an adherent to a moral perspective will not deny that there are other moral perspectives. But atheistic philosophers do not say that religious beliefs are false but that they are meaningless. Once again, their aim is to 'get somewhere', to show that there is no God. The situation is complex, for in given cases, where the conceptual analyses of religion are confused, the critics are perfectly right. But the critics show no interest in exploring alternatives, in seeing what account can be given of religious beliefs. This is because they have already sublimed the logic of our language, setting up criteria of meaningfulness that exclude religion. Think again of the way, for example, in which primitive peoples are treated as though they were primitive scientists or as the victims of superstition. We have long superseded them. The early social scientists regarded the science of culture as essentially a reformer's science. The task was to rid the world of superstition and to bring light into darkness.

What I have tried to do in my work in the philosophy of religion is to show that a sensibility should be possible there which does justice to both belief and atheism. Both are rescued from what philosophy tries to make of them. We must distinguish between the meanings of religious and atheistic perspectives and the personal appropriation of those meanings. Conceptual clarification is wider than personal appropriation. Much of contemporary philosophy of religion wants to get somewhere—to show whether there is a God. The philosophical reflection that does not go there contents itself with showing what it means to believe in God or to deny His existence. This is what I mean by a contemplative conception of philosophy, one to which I was introduced by my teachers at Swansea: J.R. Jones, R.F. Holland, Peter Winch, and Rush Rhees.

A contemplative conception of philosophy finds acceptance difficult in the present climate of Anglo-American philosophy. This is true in every field and is certainly true of the three areas in which I have concentrated my writing: philosophy of religion, ethics, and philosophy and literature. Having emphasized ethics and literature in the last two chapters, I shall confine myself in this afterword to showing this truth in relation to the philosophy of religion. What stands in the way of a contemplative conception of philosophy in contemporary philosophy of religion? The reply is four conceptions of philosophy which want to get somewhere, which are not content with contemplating where we already are.

First, a contemplative conception of philosophy is at variance with that philosophy which claims to have seen through religion. When I went to Oxford as a research student in 1958, most Oxford linguistic philosophers were of this persuasion. I would still say that the majority of philosophers look on religious belief with condescension. They may not bother to say it, but I suspect that, for them, the presence of religious belief in our culture is a hangover from a primitive state that our modernity has long superseded. It is not hard to see why a contemplative conception of philosophy is difficult to accept in such a context, for it involves getting those who think they have seen through religion to accept that they have not understood it at all. But the Wittgensteinian critique is difficult to ignore, because it does not come, as some think, from a request to do any favors for religion. It comes not from a philosopher who is an apologist for religion but from one who raised central issues in philosophical logic: issues concerning the relation of language to reality. He gave the same contemplative attention to religious discourse as he gave to other kinds of discourse. Imagine the effect on the philosophical children of the Enlightenment when Wittgenstein said that Frazer was more primitive than the primitives—that is, that the account Frazer gave of the primitives was cruder than any of the crudities he claimed to find among the primitives.

Second, a contemplative conception of philosophy falls foul of those philosophical apologists for religion who play the same game as religion's philosophical critics but who hope for the opposite results. They argue that if one is rational, one will come to see that belief in God is the best explanatory hypothesis of 'how things are' and by so doing will give a confused account of religious belief. They argue also that reflection on morality leads to religion, as though morality were a homogenous phenomenon. Thus, they fail to give the contemplative attention to other moral perspectives, including antireligious perspectives, that they deserve.

Third, a contemplative conception of philosophy creates a puzzle for some philosophical theologians who, in many ways, are sympathetic to my work. They share with me views of what I take to be confused accounts of religious belief. But, unlike me, they think these confused accounts of religion do justice to those religious beliefs which stand in need of reform. We see that religion, under the challenges of modernity, needs to be revised. And surely that is what I am doing. We are all reformers, brushing up religious language, so why can't I admit it? Reformers are people on the move—they want to get somewhere. For example, they tell us that we cannot say that God dwells on high any more. Apparently, space travel has made it impossible to speak like that.

But I am not a reformer, and I am not going anywhere. When the psalmist says that God is on high, this is not a sense to which space travel is relevant. It has more in common with the sense in which we speak of high spirits. But this does not mean that space travel cannot come between us and the language of the psalmist. It can do so by making us think that the use of 'high' in space travel *is* the only intelligible use. But it *never* did make sense to ask of the God who is said to be on high, "How high?" Our problem is, How can the Lord's song be sung in space? My fellow Welshman, the poet R. S. Thomas, has posed the issue in this way:

> What prayers will they say
> upside down in their space chambers?

It is said that explorations of this sort increase our understanding of the universe: "new conurbations a little nearer the stars." But perhaps the effect will be eroding the spiritual significance of the universe.

> ... but will there be room there
> for a garden for the Judas
> of the future to make his way through
> to give you his irradiated kiss?[2]

So I am not reforming anything, not going anywhere, but contemplating an old, old story and seeing what gets in the way of telling it today.

Fourth, I want to mention certain forms of postmodernism that are also attempts to get somewhere. Many postmodernists trace an indebtedness to Wittgenstein. Jean-François Lyotard, in *The Postmodern Condition,* makes use of Wittgenstein in his attacks on metanarratives, by which he means paradigms of discourse that are said to be the standards by which any kind of discourse must be legitimated. Lyotard points out how science has been used as such a metanarrative and how we need to be released from this and other tyrannies of language. I could not agree more. But, then, some postmodernists draw the conclusion that we create our own narratives; we decide distinctions between the real and the unreal.

2. R. S. Thomas, "What Then?" in *Mass for Hard Times* (Newcastle upon Tyne: Bloodaxe Books, 1992), p. 75.

This conclusion is deeply misleading and does not follow from anything Wittgenstein has said. In fact, philosophical hubris returns in a new form. In the old form, philosophers claimed that the rationality, epitomized by their subject, judged whether forms of discourse were well-founded. In the new form, philosophers claim to be creators of narratives that give us conceptions of reality and argue that members of the general populace, if not consciously waiting, certainly stand in need of what they have to offer. I find this a comic spectacle, and if I had to choose, I prefer the foundationalists.

But I do not have to choose, because both views are attempts to get somewhere, to say what is real or unreal. I have been contrasting such views with a contemplative conception of philosophy, one that reflects on our discourse, our understandings of the real world, endeavoring to let them be themselves in face of deep tendencies to confuse them.

Wittgenstein regarded Shakespeare with awe. He said that one could speak of Goethe's style, but not that of Shakespeare. Shakespeare shows us a world and says, "Look at it." But does not Wittgenstein too, in philosophy, attempt to show us the city with no main road—to do justice to different ways of speaking and thinking? Wittgenstein thought that this contemplative conception of philosophy is difficult to maintain in a technological culture that emphasizes finding answers and solutions, one in which 'getting somewhere' is important. A contemplative conception of philosophy, on the other hand, seeks a different kind of understanding, an understanding of the possibility of discourse. If you think from a certain angle, something must be left out. But there is a different kind of reflection characteristic of philosophy: reflection on and wonder at the fact that people do think and act from such angles with the forms of understanding they involve. Our reflections are occasioned by the puzzlements that keep recurring concerning the possibility of such understanding.

If you, as readers, have understood what I mean by a contemplative conception of philosophy, you will also understand why one of the hardest tasks in philosophy is to resist the temptation to go somewhere. Going back to the deconstructionist I mentioned at the outset, I wish I could accept his comment as a philosophical compliment without qualification. Only then could I claim to be going nowhere.

Index